First World War
and Army of Occupation
War Diary
France, Belgium and Germany

15 DIVISION
Divisional Troops
70 Brigade Royal Field Artillery
3 July 1915 - 28 February 1919

WO95/1923/3

The Naval & Military Press Ltd
www.nmarchive.com
Published in association with The National Archives

Published by

The Naval & Military Press Ltd

Unit 10 Ridgewood Industrial Park,

Uckfield, East Sussex,

TN22 5QE England

Tel: +44 (0) 1825 749494

www.naval-military-press.com

www.nmarchive.com

This diary has been reprinted in facsimile from the original. Any imperfections are inevitably reproduced and the quality may fall short of modern type and cartographic standards.

© **Crown Copyright**
Images reproduced by permission of The National Archives, London, England, 2015.

Contents

Document type	Place/Title	Date From	Date To
Heading	WO95/1923/3		
Heading	15th Division. 70th Brigade R.F.A. Jly 1915-May 1919		
Heading	15th Division. 70th Brigade R.F.A. Vol I July, Agst 9 1915		
War Diary	Bulford	03/07/1915	07/07/1915
War Diary	Horse	08/07/1915	10/07/1915
War Diary	Fourneham	10/07/1915	16/07/1915
War Diary	Gunsberque	17/07/1915	17/07/1915
War Diary	Lapugnoy	20/07/1915	28/07/1915
War Diary	Mazingarbe	29/07/1915	31/08/1915
Heading	War Diary. Headquarters. 70th Brigade R.F.A. (15th Division) September 1915		
War Diary	Mazingarbe	01/09/1915	25/09/1915
War Diary	Philosophe	26/09/1915	30/09/1915
Heading	15th Division. 70th Bde. R.F.A. Vol 2 Oct 15		
War Diary	Philosophe	01/10/1915	02/10/1915
War Diary	Houchin	03/10/1915	03/10/1915
War Diary	Lapugnoy	04/10/1915	15/10/1915
War Diary	Mazingarbe	16/10/1915	31/10/1915
Heading	15th Division. 70th Bde. R.F.A. Vol 3. Nov 15		
War Diary	Marzingarbe	01/11/1915	22/11/1915
War Diary	Vermelles	23/11/1915	30/11/1915
Heading	15th Div. 70th Bde. R.F.A. Vol 4		
War Diary	Vermelles	16/12/1915	16/12/1915
War Diary	Marles-les-Mines	17/12/1915	31/12/1915
Heading	70th Bde R.F.A. Vol 5 Jan 16		
War Diary	Marles-les-Mines	01/01/1916	05/01/1916
War Diary	Letermans	06/01/1916	07/01/1916
War Diary	Marles-les-Mines	08/01/1916	15/01/1916
War Diary	Mazingarbe	16/01/1916	16/04/1916
War Diary	Ecquedecques	17/04/1916	28/04/1916
War Diary	Vemelles	29/04/1916	30/04/1916
War Diary	Philosophe	01/05/1916	31/05/1916
Heading	War Diary C/70th Brigade R.F.A. May 1916		
War Diary	Annequin	01/05/1916	31/05/1916
War Diary Miscellaneous	Vermelles	01/05/1916	30/06/1916
War Diary	Vermelles	01/06/1916	04/06/1916
War Diary	Verquigneul	05/06/1916	20/06/1916
Heading	War Diary C/70th Brigade R.F.A. June 1916		
War Diary	Vermelles	01/06/1916	30/06/1916
Heading	70th Bde. R.F.A. Vol 6		
Miscellaneous	H.Q. 15th Div. arty.	31/07/1916	31/07/1916
War Diary	Field	01/07/1916	31/07/1916
Operation(al) Order(s)	Operation Order No 1 70th Brigade, R.F.A.	25/07/1916	25/07/1916
Miscellaneous	Operation Order. 70th Brigade, R.F.A.	26/07/1916	26/07/1916
Miscellaneous	Operation Order. 70th Brigade, R.F.A.	28/07/1916	28/07/1916
Miscellaneous	Operation Order. 70th Brigade. R.F.A.	30/07/1916	30/07/1916
Miscellaneous	A/70th Bde R.F.A. July 1st-July 29th	01/07/1916	01/07/1916
War Diary	War Diary D/70th Brigade R.F.A. July 1916		

Miscellaneous	To HQ 70th Bde.	01/07/1916	01/07/1916
Miscellaneous	From OC Div To HQ 70th Bde.	01/07/1916	01/07/1916
War Diary	Field	01/07/1916	20/07/1916
Heading	15th Divisional Artillery. 70th Brigade Royal Field Artillery. August 1916		
Heading	War Diary of 70th Brigade R.F.A. from 1st August, 1916 to 31st August. 1916 Volume Number 14		
Miscellaneous	H. Qrs 15th DA HQ.8	31/08/1916	31/08/1916
War Diary	Field	01/08/1916	31/08/1916
Miscellaneous	Operation Order. 70th Brigade. R.F.A.		
Miscellaneous	Operation Order. 70th Brigade, R.F.A.	01/08/1916	01/08/1916
Miscellaneous	Operation Order. 70th Brigade, R.F.A.		
Miscellaneous	70th Brigade R.F.A. for information	01/08/1916	01/08/1916
Operation(al) Order(s)	15th D.A. Operation Order No. 31	02/08/1916	02/08/1916
Miscellaneous	March Table for 3rd August to accompany 15th D.A. O.O. No. 31		
Miscellaneous	War Diary C/70th Brigade R.F.A. September 1916		
Miscellaneous	To. H.Q. XV D.A. C.R. 31		
Heading	War Diary of 70th Brigade Royal Field Arty From 1st September, 1916 to 30th September, 1916 Volume Number 15		
War Diary		04/09/1916	28/09/1916
War Diary	In the Field	29/09/1916	30/09/1916
War Diary	Field	01/09/1916	03/09/1916
War Diary	In The Field	02/09/1916	20/09/1916
War Diary	Frechencourt	01/09/1916	01/09/1916
War Diary	Malboro Wood (Catepillar Valley)	02/09/1916	11/09/1916
War Diary	Contalmaison	12/09/1916	14/09/1916
War Diary	Contalmaison Villa	15/09/1916	20/09/1916
Heading	War Diary D/70th Brigade R.F.A. October 1916		
Heading	War Diary of 70 Bde RFA. 1st October, 1916 to 31st October, 1916 Volume. 16		
War Diary	Bazentine Le Petit	01/10/1916	04/10/1916
War Diary	St Gratien	04/10/1916	16/10/1916
War Diary	Contalmaison Villa	17/10/1916	31/10/1916
War Diary	Martin Puich	04/10/1916	18/10/1916
Heading	War Diary of 70th Bde RFA From 1st November, 1916-30th November, 1916 Volume 17		
Miscellaneous	Head. In 15th. Divl. Arty.	30/11/1916	30/11/1916
War Diary	Contalmaison Villa	01/11/1916	16/11/1916
War Diary	Pierregot Contalmaison villa	17/11/1916	30/11/1916
Heading	War Diary of 70th Brigade R.F.A. From 1st December, 1916 to 31st December, 1916. Volume 18		
War Diary	Field	01/12/1916	31/12/1916
War Diary	Martin Puich	22/12/1916	31/12/1916
Heading	War Diary of 70th Brigade R.F.A. 1st January 1917-31st January 1917. Volume 19		
War Diary	Pierregot Bazentin. Le. Petit	01/01/1917	16/01/1917
War Diary	Bazentin Le Petit	16/01/1917	31/01/1917
War Diary	Field	06/01/1917	17/01/1917
War Diary	S 3c 7.8	05/01/1917	30/01/1917
Heading	War Diary of 70th. Brigade R.F.A. 15th. Divisional Artillery for month of February 1917. Volume XX		
War Diary	Bazentin Le Petit	01/02/1917	05/02/1917
War Diary	Molliens au Bois	06/02/1917	15/02/1917
War Diary	Occoches	16/02/1917	16/02/1917

War Diary	Boubers	17/02/1917	17/02/1917
War Diary	St. Michel	18/02/1917	25/02/1917
War Diary	Arras	26/02/1917	28/02/1917
Heading	War Diary of 70th Bde. R.F.A. From 1st March 1917-To 31st March 1917 Volume 21		
War Diary	St. Michel and Arras	01/03/1917	07/03/1917
War Diary	Duisans	08/03/1917	11/03/1917
War Diary	Arras	16/03/1917	09/04/1917
War Diary	Feuchy	10/04/1917	30/04/1917
Heading	War Diary of 70th Brigade R.F.A. from 1st May, 1917. to 31st May, 1917. Volume 23		
War Diary	Tilloy	01/05/1917	23/05/1917
War Diary	Laitre St. Quentin	24/05/1917	24/05/1917
War Diary	Rebreuviette.	25/05/1917	25/05/1917
War Diary	Conchy-S-Conche	26/05/1917	26/05/1917
War Diary	Conchy-Sur-Conche	27/05/1917	31/05/1917
Heading	War Diary of 70th Brigade, R.F.A. From 1st June, 1917. To 30th June 1917 Volume 24		
War Diary	Conchy-Sur-Conche	01/06/1917	15/06/1917
War Diary	Heuchin	16/06/1917	16/06/1917
War Diary	Norrent Fontes	17/06/1917	17/06/1917
War Diary	Thiennes	18/06/1917	19/06/1917
War Diary	Godewaersvelde	20/06/1917	20/06/1917
War Diary	Watou	21/06/1917	24/06/1917
War Diary	Ypres	25/06/1917	30/06/1917
Heading	War Diary of 70th Brigade R.F.A. From 1st October 1917 To 31st October 1917 (Volume 28)		
War Diary	Athies	01/10/1917	31/10/1917
Heading	War Diary of 70th Brigade R.F.A. (Volume 28) From 1st November 1917. To 30th November 1917		
War Diary	Arras	01/11/1917	14/11/1917
War Diary	Beaulen Court	15/11/1917	15/11/1917
War Diary	Bus	16/11/1917	19/11/1917
War Diary	Havrincourt Wood Metz	20/11/1917	20/11/1917
War Diary	Flesquieres	21/11/1917	30/11/1917
Heading	War Diary of 70th Brigade R.F.A. (Volume 29). From 1st December 1917 to 31st December 1917		
War Diary	Gouzeaucourt Wood	01/12/1917	18/12/1917
War Diary	Sorel Le Grand	19/12/1917	20/12/1917
War Diary	Arras	21/12/1917	31/12/1917
Heading	War Diary of 70th Brigade R.F.A. (Volume 30).From 1st January 1918 To 31st January 1918		
War Diary	Athies	01/01/1918	04/01/1918
War Diary	Harbarcq	05/01/1918	31/01/1918
Heading	War Diary of 70th Brigade R.F.A. Volume 31. From 1st February 1918. To 1st March 1918		
War Diary	Habarcq	01/02/1918	07/02/1918
War Diary	Monchy	08/02/1918	28/02/1918
Heading	15th Divisional Artillery. 70th Brigade R.F.A. March 1918		
Heading	War Diary of 70th Brigade R.F.A. (Volume 32) From 1st March 1918. to 31st March 1918		
War Diary	Monchy	01/03/1918	31/03/1918
Heading	15th Divisional Artillery War Diary 70th Brigade R.F.A. April 1918		

Heading	War Diary of 70th Brigade R.F.A. (Volume 33).from 1st April 1918 To 30th April 1918		
War Diary		01/04/1918	30/04/1918
Heading	War Diary of 70th Brigade R.F.A. (Volume 34) From 1st May 1918 To 31st May 1918		
War Diary		01/05/1918	28/05/1918
War Diary	Roclincourt	29/05/1918	31/05/1918
Heading	War Diary of 70th Brigade R.F.A. (Volume 35) From 1st June 1918. To 30th June 1918		
War Diary	Roclincourt	01/06/1918	18/06/1918
War Diary	Blangy Ecurie	19/06/1918	22/06/1918
War Diary	Blangy	23/06/1918	23/06/1918
War Diary	Chateau	24/06/1918	25/06/1918
War Diary	Arras	26/06/1918	30/06/1918
Heading	War Diary of 70th Brigade R.F.A. (Volume 36.) From 1st July 1918 To 31st July 1918		
War Diary	Arras	01/07/1918	14/07/1918
War Diary	Acq	15/07/1918	19/07/1918
War Diary	Vieux Moulin	20/07/1918	20/07/1918
War Diary	Morte Fontaine	21/07/1918	21/07/1918
War Diary	Stpierre Aigle	22/07/1918	23/07/1918
War Diary	Chaudin	28/07/1918	31/07/1918
Heading	War Diary of 70th Brigade R.F.A. From 1st August 1918. To 31st August 1918 (Volume 37)		
War Diary	Chaudun	01/08/1918	02/08/1918
War Diary	Dommiers	03/08/1918	03/08/1918
War Diary	Rally	04/08/1918	04/08/1918
War Diary	Ligneville	05/08/1918	05/08/1918
War Diary	Etree Wamin	06/08/1918	17/08/1918
War Diary	Agny	17/08/1918	25/08/1918
War Diary	Tilloy	26/08/1918	26/08/1918
War Diary	N 16 (map 51 NW)	27/08/1918	28/08/1918
War Diary	Wamcourt	29/08/1918	31/08/1918
Heading	War Diary of 70th Brigade R.F.A. (Volume 38) From 1st September 1918. To 30th September 1918		
War Diary	Valley of the Sensee	01/09/1918	01/09/1918
War Diary	Boiry S.E	02/09/1918	05/09/1918
War Diary	Arras Hersin	06/08/1918	30/08/1918
Heading	War Diary of 70th Brigade R.F.A. From 1/10/18 to 31/10/18		
War Diary	Loos Elevaston Castle	01/10/1918	12/10/1918
War Diary	Elvaston Castle	13/10/1918	15/10/1918
War Diary	Vendin	15/10/1918	15/10/1918
War Diary	Quarry I 2000-80	16/10/1918	16/10/1918
War Diary	Quarry I20c (44a) and Libercourt	17/10/1918	17/10/1918
War Diary	Libercourt and Drumez	18/10/1918	18/10/1918
War Diary	Laverderie	19/10/1918	19/10/1918
War Diary	Laverderie Cenech Chateau and Bercu	20/10/1918	20/10/1918
War Diary	Bercu-Petit Runes (44 S. 7.a)	21/10/1918	31/10/1918
Heading	War Diary of 70th Brigade R.F.A. (Volume 40) From 1st November 1918. To 30th November 1918		
War Diary	Petit Rumes	01/11/1918	08/11/1918
War Diary	Wis Velvin	09/11/1918	09/11/1918
War Diary	Antoing	10/11/1918	10/11/1918
War Diary	Tourpes	11/11/1918	11/11/1918
War Diary	Ormeignies	12/11/1918	20/11/1918

War Diary	Jardin	21/11/1918	30/11/1918
Heading	War Diary of 70th Brigade R.F.A. (Volume 41) From 1st December 1918. To 31st December 1918		
War Diary	Jardin	01/12/1918	17/12/1918
War Diary	Horres	18/12/1918	18/12/1918
War Diary	Rebecq	19/12/1918	31/12/1918
Heading	War Diary of 70th Brigade R.F.A. (Volume 42) From 1st January 1919. To 31st January		
War Diary	Rebecq	01/01/1919	31/01/1919
Heading	War Diary of 70th Brigade R.F.A. (Volume 43) From 1st February 1919. To 28th February 1919		
War Diary	Rebecq	01/02/1919	28/02/1919
Heading	War Diary of 70th Brigade R.F.A. (Volume 44) From 1st March 1919 To 31st March 1919		
War Diary	Rebecq-Rognon (Belgium)	00/03/1919	00/03/1919
Heading	War Diary of 70th Brigade R.F.A. (Volume 45) From 1st April To 30th April 1919		
War Diary	Rebecq-Rognon (Belgium)	00/04/1919	00/05/1919

mom 5:45 (9:38)

mom 5:45 (9:38)

15TH DIVISION

70TH BRIGADE R.F.A.

JLY 1915 - MAY 1919

121/7050

15th Division

70th Brigade R.F.A.
Vol I
July, Aug & Sep 1915
1915

Army Form C. 2118.

4th DF Bde R.F.A

WAR DIARY
or
INTELLIGENCE SUMMARY.
(Erase heading not required.)

Instructions regarding War Diaries and Intelligence Summaries are contained in F. S. Regs., Part II. and the Staff Manual respectively. Title pages will be prepared in manuscript.

Place	Date	Hour	Summary of Events and Information	Remarks and references to Appendices
Bulford	3/7/15	11.h.M	Received orders to hold the Brigade in readiness to embark at SOUTHAMPTON on 7/7/15	WD
-do-	7/7/15	9 P.M.	Left in eleven trains, Entrained at SOUTHAMPTON. H.Q. 4, 1/2 B, 1/2 C Bty in S.S. INVENTOR	WD
Harve	8/7/15	7 A.M.	anchored off SPITHEAD. Remainder of Bde sailed to HARVE. Disembarked at HARVE. D/70 & Bde Am Col entrained for AUDRIQUE. 1/2 A, 1/2 B	WD
Harve	9/7/15	7 A.M.	1/2 C Btys went to CAMP 5. H.Q., 1/2 A, 1/2 B, 1/2 C Btys arrived and disembarked, remained at Docks until 5 P.M. then entrained left HARVE at 8 P.M.	WD
	10/7/15	2.30 p.h.	Arrived at AUDRIQUE. Marched 6 miles to TOURNEHEM. Billeted men in Barns horses & guns in Orchards. Remained in billets until 15/7/15 (Tetanus)	WD
Tournehem	15/7/15	9 A.M.	Marched to COMPAGNE. Billeted. Horse destroyed	WD
-do-	16/7/15	7 A.M.	D: Moncrieff B/70 Drowned in Canal body not recovered, 12 Noon marched to GUARBICQUE. Billeted in Barns	WD
Guarbecque	17/7/15	9 A.M.	Marched to LAPUGNOY. Billeted in Barns, Guns & Horses in Fields, remained there until 29/7/15	WD
Lapugny	29/7/15	9 P.M.	The Right section from A, C & D Btys were attached to 1st Div in action for instruction for a period of 96 hours	WD

1577 Wt. W10791/1773 500,000 1/15 D. D. & L. A.D.S.S./Forms/C. 2118.

Y.D. Bde R.F.A.

Army Form C. 2118.

WAR DIARY
or
INTELLIGENCE SUMMARY.
(Erase heading not required.)

Place	Date	Hour	Summary of Events and Information	Remarks and references to Appendices
LAPUGNOY	July 1915 24th	9 p.m.	Y.L. Left section of H, L, & D Btys relieved their Right Section for period of 96 hours for instruction	MD
- do -	27th	9 p.m.	The Right Section of H L Bty relieved one section 14th Lon Bty for registration at MAZINGARBE.	MD
- do -	28th	9.30 p.m	Left Sections of H.L. & D. Btys moved from 1st Div area and took up position in action in 47th Div area at MAZINGARBE. L Section with their R section. E. Bty left section relieved one section 13th Lon Bty. "D" left relieved one section 17th Lon Bty.	MD
- do -	"	10 p.m.	Right Section B Bty was attached to 51st Bde R.F.A. for instruction for 96 hours. Left Sec B Bty it section moved from LAPUGNOY into position with their I section	
MAZINGARBE	29th	10 p.m.	at MAZINGARBE	MD
- do -	30th	5 p.m.	H & D Btys completed their registration on LOOS	MD
		6.30 p.m	2nd Lieut E.Y.O wounded on G.H. Bty & one 9th L Bty wounded	MD
- do -	31st		H.L. & D. Battery occupying position taken over from 5th Lon Bde R.F.A.(T.F.) at the head of new trench 140th Bde R.F.A. on Right & 41st Bde R.F.A. on Left. 144th Inf Bde occupy my trenches in our immediate front. Batteries opened retaliatory fire on enemy positions at various times during the day. No casualties. 2nd Lt Early Bde A.m. Col joined in relief of 2nd Lt Quickly wounded on 30th inst.	

70th By R.F.A.

WAR DIARY
or
INTELLIGENCE SUMMARY
(Erase heading not required.)

Army Form C. 2118.

Instructions regarding War Diaries and Intelligence Summaries are contained in F. S. Regs., Part II. and the Staff Manual respectively. Title pages will be prepared in manuscript.

Place	Date	Hour	Summary of Events and Information	Remarks and references to Appendices
MAZINGARBE	Aug 1st		Little activity on our front. No 2 Battery fired a few retaliatory rounds D/B/g. Shelled enemy's working party at 9.45 P.M. dispersing it. Enemy shelled MAZINGARBE at 5.30 P.M. Two charges of T.E. ARNOLD B Battery. Two charges of H.E. shell into MAROC. B Battery man killed. Weather good.	N/R
-do-	2nd	6 P.M.	Enemy fired a few H.E. shell into MAROC. D Bty replying on LOOS church. N/R 2 O/R killed enemy trench trip by numbers. Enemy's result in N/R. Sun + line spasmodic. Various enemy working parties were dispersed. Weather most oppressive. Typhoons.	N/R
-do-	3rd	4.30	Enemy commenced shelling A/Battery north of MAROC. D Bty replying on LOOS. N/R	
			Our Forward trench attacked by enemy. 7 P.M. D Battery assisted by night. N/R	
			So actively in our front by J.A. & D. Batteries continue to N/R	
			reply. Our gun pits dug out. An enemy platoon was	
			firing. Aug 4th 9 P.M. Enemy search for batteries using guns	
-do-	5th	3:30 P.M.	Enemy platoon in my front line trenches and billets in MAROC. N/R	
			L.13 fired in retaliation in the neighbourhood of LOOS. Information N/R	
			was made by telephone communication + Gul Pits	

WAR DIARY or INTELLIGENCE SUMMARY

Army Form C. 2118.

70th Bde R.F.A.

Place	Date	Hour	Summary of Events and Information	Remarks and references to Appendices
MAZINGARBE	Aug 6th	9.0 AM	Enemy fired a few rounds on our billets in MAROC with H.E. Shells.	
	7th		B/190 retaliated with B/70 Bns & Ins. Enemy continues to prepare new Bttys. 9th Coy R.E. gave instructions for preparing emery sapping (?)	
-do-	7th	3.5 pm	Enemy shelled our infantry trenches, C. Bty fired a few retaliatory rounds.	
			In the vicinity of LOOS CHURCH, otherwise quiet.	
-do-	8th	6.5 pm	Enemy fired a few rounds on MAROC. D. Bty retaliated on LOOS Sunken Rd	
	9th		Enemy Heavy Bty firing seven shells into MAROC & H.E.(?)	
		2 pm	Aeroplane on Obsn Duty (?) trenches in LOOS.	
-do-	10th	6.30 pm	C. Bty fired 6 rounds on enemy working parties at LOOS and North.	
	11th	7.45 am	Enemy fired several shells of two kinds Nysthyn (?) Bty into MAROC, 7 H.E.(?)	
		10 AM	Enemy heavy gun again fired into MAROC Church.	
		1.55 pm	D. Bty fired on reply as at the request of Infantry Comdt.	
-do-	12th	2.5 pm	Enemy gun fired a few H.E. shell into MAROC. B. Bty retaliated on LOOS.	
		4 pm	Enemy going out to repair Telephone wire found a civilian handing (?)	
			over our Comdt & said that killing the civilian who was handing over to Enemy Bty D.	

Army Form C. 2118.

H.Q. 4th Bde R.F.A.
h 40= Bac R.F.A.

WAR DIARY
or
INTELLIGENCE SUMMARY.
(Erase heading not required.)

Instructions regarding War Diaries and Intelligence Summaries are contained in F. S. Regs., Part II. and the Staff Manual respectively. Title pages will be prepared in manuscript.

Place	Date	Hour	Summary of Events and Information	Remarks and references to Appendices
	AUG?			
MAZINGARBE	13th	6 p.m.	6/73rd Bac fired on SAP on the LENS ROAD, on enemy fell short and rear our infantry trenches, fire was stopped by O.C. 70 Bac and ordered to add 25.0 yds to range	WD
–do–	14th	9.30 a.m.	Enemy fired on our infantry trenches. A, B, & D Batteries fires a few retaliation rounds. 10.15 A.m. D Bty fired on enemy trenches. Heavy Aerial Observation which was very successful	WD
–do–	15th	P.M. 5.30	Hostile Batteries fired on our infantry trenches. A Bty retaliating weather showery. Observation difficult	WD
–do–	16th	5 p.m.	Enemy shelled our infantry trenches from the vicinity of LOOS. A Bty retaliated, snipers were active at 8.45 p.m. C Bty whilst trying to get into communication by Lamp from Observation station at MAROC were fired on by snipers in the vicinity of MAROC CHURCH. 9.30 p.m. B Bty from usual NOEUX LE MINES Reserve A Bty	WD
–do–	17th	1.15 A.m	Gun Team of Bac Ion Column was killed by lightning. Enemy fired on our infantry trenches several times during the day B, C, & D Btys retaliating. Weather Bad. Observation difficult.	WD
–do–	18th	9.35	Enemy Artillery Active intermittently on our infantry trenches	WD

90th Bde R.F.A.

Army Form C. 2118.

WAR DIARY
or
INTELLIGENCE SUMMARY.
(Erase heading not required.)

Instructions regarding War Diaries and Intelligence Summaries are contained in F. S. Regs., Part II. and the Staff Manual respectively. Title pages will be prepared in manuscript.

Place	Date	Hour	Summary of Events and Information	Remarks and references to Appendices
MAZINGARBE	August 18th		from the direction of LOOS. N.By retaliating on their Sy trenches, thereafter Bde withdrawals owing to Mist.	A.P.D.
–do–	19th	5.30pm	Enemy line turned shell into hilltop at MAROC. C.By retaliated on hostile in LOOS. otherwise all quiet on our front.	A.P.D.
–do–	20th	6.p.m.	Enemy fired a few shells on our infantry trenches. D.By retaliating. Slight front trenches. weather misty, observation difficult.	A.P.D.
–do–	21st	9.pm	Enemy very quiet on our front	A.P.D.
–do–	22nd	8.20pm	Enemy shelled our front line trenches. B/By fired a few retaliatory rounds	A.P.D.
–do–	23rd	4.30pm	Enemy turn fired several shells into GRENAY. B/By retaliating on their front line trenches W LOOS	A.P.D.
–do–	24th	5.pm	Enemy shells hillock in MAROC. D.By retaliated on hostile in LOOS	A.P.D.
–do–	25th	2.30am	Enemy fired on our infantry front line trenches. 90 Bde retaliating on sy front trenches	A.P.D.
–do–	26		Everything quiet on our immediate front. 9.p.m. 31.By came into action from reserve at AUDRICOURT. & relieved C.By who went back to Reserve at DOUVRIN.	A.P.D.
–do–	27th		Little activity on our immediate front	A.P.D.

1577 Wt. W10791/1773 500,000 1/15 D. D. & L. A.D.S.S./Forms/C. 2118.

WAR DIARY or INTELLIGENCE SUMMARY.

Army Form C. 2118

70th Bde R.F.A.

(Erase heading not required.)

Place	Date	Hour	Summary of Events and Information	Remarks and references to Appendices
MAZINGARBE	AUG 28th 1915.	11.15 AM	Enemy fired on Pullets in MAROC. B Bty retaliating on Pullets in LOOS.	AAA.
— do —	29th	2.30 PM	Little activity on our immediate front. A & D Batteries fired a few retaliatory rounds on enemy's trench in LOOS.	AAA
— do —	30th	5 PM	Enemy shells on my trench. D Bty retaliating on thy trench	AAA
— do —	31st	4.50 AM	A, B, & D Batteries fired on LOOS in retaliation for firing on MAROC	AAA

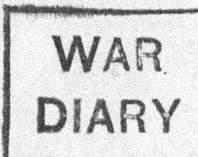

Headquarters,

70th BRIGADE, R.F.A.

(15th Division)

S E P T E M B E R

1 9 1 5

40th Bde R.F.A.

WAR DIARY
or
INTELLIGENCE SUMMARY.
(Erase heading not required.)

Army Form C. 2118.

Sept 1915

Place	Date	Hour	Summary of Events and Information	Remarks and references to Appendices
MAZINGARBE	Sept 1st		Enemy fires intermittently on billets in MAROC. D. Bty fires a few retaliatory rounds	
- do -	2nd		Little activity on our front, new emplacements are being made for B & C Batteries about 300 yds W of present position. Weather dull & difficult	
- do -	3rd		Enemy fires a few rounds on our infantry trenches from the direction of LOOS. D. Bty retaliating on their trenches. Weather dull & dry	
- do -	4th	10 p.m	B & C Batteries moved into new positions 300 yds W of old position	
- do -	5th	5 p.m	Little activity on our immediate front. B, B, & C Batteries fire a few rounds in retaliation on billets in LOOS.	
- do -	6th		Enemy firing intermittently on our infantry trenches. D. Bty retaliating on enemy trenches	
- do -	7th		Little activity on our immediate front, observation difficulty	
- do -	8th		Enemy fired a few rounds on our trenches at various times during the night	
- do -	9th		Little activity on our immediate front	
- do -	10th		Enemy fires intermittently on our trenches. D. Bty fires a few retaliatory rounds	

Army Form C. 2118.

40th Bn R.F.A.

WAR DIARY
or
INTELLIGENCE SUMMARY.

(Erase heading not required.)

Instructions regarding War Diaries and Intelligence Summaries are contained in F. S. Regs., Part II. and the Staff Manual respectively. Title pages will be prepared in manuscript.

Place	Date	Hour	Summary of Events and Information	Remarks and references to Appendices
MAZINGARBE	Sept 11	6 p.m.	Registered whole battery on our immediate front & R.O. fired a few rounds in retaliation.	R.O.
— do —	12	—	Gun very dull – no work	R.O.
— do —	12	11 am	Battery enemy front line turned as ordered. No reply	R.O.
— do —	13	3 p.m.	Enemy shelled lines in our trenches & R.O. retaliated on them	R.O.
			Enemy Howitzer fired 80 rounds — no damage	R.O.
— do —	14–15		Intermittently on our front by R.O. Battery fired a few retaliatory shots	R.O.
— do —	15		Enemy trench mortars dropped bombs on our vicinity. Battery fired 8 rounds on E.R.B. without any damage being done to retaliate	R.O.
— do —	15–16		on enemy trenches	R.O.
— do —	16		R.O. killed our Trenches in the direction of LOOS. Also carried on harassing fire on our Front line	R.O.
— do —	17		Much activity on our Front line	R.O.
— do —	18		Systematic shelling of P+LOS positions in the direction of MILLUCH	R.O.
— do —	18–19		Enemy continually shelled the night 18th/19th Sept. No further action	R.O.
— do —	19	8 a.m.	Enemy fired a few rounds in the vicinity of MAZINGARBE Battery retaliating	R.O.
— do —	20	9 f.	Received orders to take part in the Bombardment which is to take place on the 21/9/15	R.O.

1577 Wt. W10791/1773 500,000 1/15 D. D. & L. A.D.S.S./Forms/C. 2118.

90th Bde R.F.A

Army Form C. 2118.

WAR DIARY
or
INTELLIGENCE SUMMARY.
(Erase heading not required.)

Instructions regarding War Diaries and Intelligence Summaries are contained in F. S. Regs., Part II. and the Staff Manual respectively. Title pages will be prepared in manuscript.

Place	Date	Hour	Summary of Events and Information	Remarks and references to Appendices
MAZINGARBE	Sept 1915 21st	7 a.m.	The Brigade was allotted a frontage of 800 yards of wire to be cut, which was divided between A, B, & D Batteries. The position of the wire was 1850 yards N.W. of LOOS CHURCH and 200 yds N of the LENS — BETHUNE Road. Range 3100. A & D Batteries were engaged on the wire from 7 to 8 a.m. Observation very difficult, being done with Periscopes from the front line trenches. 7.90 8.a.m. B, & C. Batteries were engaged on the enemy's strong point with H.E. Their A & D Batteries and B & C Batteries fired on wire & strong point alternately during the day. Progress of the wire satisfactory, several gaps being cut through round by D. expended 1,687 shrapnel. H.E. 197.	
—do—	22nd	7.0 h.	A, B, C, D Batteries engaged on wire cutting from 7 a.m to 6 p.m, enemy attempts to have repaired wire of their own during the night— they were shelled by B, B by's Wipers. Letter T.E.O. Chambridges slightly wounded. also doing day rounds expended 1655 shrapnel & H.E. 262 H.E.	
—do—	23rd	7 a.m.	A, B, C, & D Batteries continued to cut wire which was allotted them, in the B.D. cut, also fired on enemy strong point, at various Ranges and T.H. & other progress on wire very satisfactory being little retaliation from the enemy rounds expended shrapnel 1895, High Explosive 299. wire left good.	

Army Form C. 2118.

70. G. Bde. R.F.A.

WAR DIARY
or
INTELLIGENCE SUMMARY.

(Erase heading not required.)

Instructions regarding War Diaries and Intelligence Summaries are contained in F.S. Regs., Part II. and the Staff Manual respectively. Title pages will be prepared in manuscript.

Place	Date	Hour	Summary of Events and Information	Remarks and references to Appendices
MAZINGARBE	Sept 24th	4.30 p.m.	A/B, C, & D Batteries completed wire cutting which appeared to be satisfactory as far as can be observed from front line. Hundred (?) rounds of 6 p.m. received Gas Zylyn (?) orders starting time of attack to take place at 5.50 A.m. on the 25th. Life (?) rounds expended during the day 1773. Shot fired 336 H.E.	
MAZINGARBE	25th	5.30 a.m.	The Brigade received orders to fire on enemy's second line trenched W. of LOOS. running from LOOS CEMETERY to 1000 yards Northwards, fire commenced at 5.30 a.m. & kept up until 6.30 a.m. range 3800 yards. At 6.40 a.m. B.A.H. received orders to lift their fire on to CHALKPIT WOOD 2000 yards E. of their first objective. A & D Batteries to lift on to LOOS and search road E. of LOOS fire was kept up for 25 minutes at various ranges, they then ceased firing, at 10.a.m. 69 B. Batteries advanced about 1 mile and took up position in action North of MAROC to cover advance of 4th Infantry Bde. who were advancing towards HILL 70. at 3 p.m. A & D Batteries advanced & moved into action to position in the wood. B & C Batteries remained there that day. The Brigade Comry Staff. Mon forward into LOOS with Headquarters of 44 Inf Bde. as reconnoitre a position for the Bde. but owing to the confusion on	

1577 Wt. W10791/1773 500,000 1/15 D. D. & L. A.D.S.S./Forms/C. 2118.

WAR DIARY or INTELLIGENCE SUMMARY

Army Form C. 2118.

40th Bde R.F.A.

Place	Date	Hour	Summary of Events and Information	Remarks and references to Appendices
	Sept 1915 25		our left being held up it was found impossible to advance the battery further forward as LOOS was being enfiladed from the direction of HULLUCH and LENS. Rounds expended 2507 shrapnel + 189 HE. Blue weather wet cold and misty + raining.	A.F.D.
PHILOSOPHE	26		15th Division were to attack HILL 70 Redoubt at 9 a.m. A & B Batteries established a barrage (shrapnel) on a line E of HILL 70. Rate of fire 2 rounds per battery per minute from 8.30 to 9.30 a.m. at 9.30 a.m. lifted to CITE ST AUGUSTE. Slower rate of fire (20 per cent HE Shell) until 10 a.m. B & C Batteries were ready to open fire on HULLUCH 9.45 a.m. received orders for B & C Batteries to open fire on HULLUCH from 10 to 11 a.m. rate of fire one round per gun per minute. Casualties 2nd Lieut W.N. ARNOLD wounded. Other ranks 1 Driver Killed and 9 wounded. Rounds expended 2791 shrapnel, 136 HE + blue. Weather fair. Brigade Headquarters established at PHILOSOPHE J.D.	A.F.D.
PHILOSOPHE	27		unable to advance owing to counter attacks by the enemy on HILL 70. The batteries did little during the day, most of day was breaking up emplacements. Major M.R. COURAGE wounded by sniper in leg. Other ranks wounded 3. Weather fair.	A.F.D.

1577 Wt. W10791/1773 500,000 1/15 D. D. & L.   A.D.S.S./Forms/C. 2118.

40th Bde R.F.A.

Army Form C. 2118.

WAR DIARY
or
INTELLIGENCE SUMMARY.
(Erase heading not required.)

Place	Date	Hour	Summary of Events and Information	Remarks and references to Appendices
PHILOSOPHE	Sept 1915. 28th		No firing done during the day. Improvised gunpits & shelters for the men 5th were ordered to batteries to establish a barrage 300 yards S.E. of HILL 70. 9 improvised gunpits to search back to CITÉ ST AUGUSTE and woods N. of it. Rounds allowed per hour 18. Guns to be maintained until 5.30 a.m. on the 29th. Not rounds expended. 2.33 Shrapnel 1308 H.E. Shell.	
—do—	29th		Artillery occupying the same position. Did no firing. MJR C.P. CULLERNE wounded by sniper	
	30"		No firing took place by the batteries during the day which was occupied by improving gunpits. Capt. E.G. HATFIELD was attached to the command of J.H. Battery in place of MJR M.R. COURAGE wounded on 29th inst.	

121/7592

15th Division

70th Bde: R.F.A.
Vol 2
Oct 15

WAR DIARY
or
INTELLIGENCE SUMMARY

Army Form C. 2118.

(Erase heading not required.)

Place	Date	Hour	Summary of Events and Information	Remarks and references to Appendices
PHILOSOPHE	October 1915 1st		MJR. C.P. CULLERNE, 2nd LIEUT W.N. ARNOLD joined & the strength of the Brigade	
		10 p.m	D Battery and right section of A.B.Y & Batteries were relieved by the FRENCH ARTILLERY. They then proceeded to HOUCHIN in reserve	A/P.D
—do—	2nd	8 p.m	The left section of A.B.Y. & were relieved by the FRENCH. The section then joined their respective Batteries at HOUCHIN.	A/P.D
HOUCHIN	3rd	10.30 am	Received orders for the Brigade to march to LAPUGNOY at 5 p.m. and billeted the men in barns. Horses & Guns were parked in fields. Capts. G.E. KIDD & E. BOYCE joined the Brigade and took over A.B.Y. & Batteries respectively	A/P.D
LAPUGNOY	4th		General overhauling of Guns, General repairing harness & saddles, buffer springs &c. MR. CROVES, NJR. M.R. COURAGE, Luncheon of the String M/D.	A/P.D
—do—	5th		Overhauling of Guns & Carriages etc	A/P.D
—do—	6th		Harness Cleaning & Repairing	A/P.D
—do—	7th		Drivers Drill. Signalling. Rifle Drill	A/P.D
—do—	8th		—do—	A/P.D
—do—	9th		—do—	A/P.D
—do—	10th			A/P.D
—do—	11th		Received orders to hold the Brigade in readiness to move at an hours notice. Instructions telephone communication	A/P.D

70th A Bde R.F.A.
20th Division

WAR DIARY
or
INTELLIGENCE SUMMARY.
(Erase heading not required.)

Army Form C. 2118.

Instructions regarding War Diaries and Intelligence Summaries are contained in F.S. Regs., Part II. and the Staff Manual respectively. Title pages will be prepared in manuscript.

Place	Date	Hour	Summary of Events and Information	Remarks and references to Appendices
LAPUGNOY	October 1915. 12th	A.M. 10:50	Received 15th Divn Operation order No 13.	AyD
— do —	13th		Gun, Rifle, & Stores Drive. Instructions in cable laying.	AyD
— do —	14th	6 p.m.	Received orders to move one section of each battery into action in the vicinity of PHILOSOPHE on the 15th inst.	AyD
— do —	15th	3 p.m.	One section of A.B, C. & D. Batteries moved into action 1000 yards S.E. of PHILOSOPHE.	AyD
MAZINGARBE	16th	3 p.m.	Remaining sections of A.B, C, D. Batteries moved into action with the sections already in action on the 15th inst. a few rounds were registered on the German lines, rounds expended 128. Brigade Headquarters at MAZINGARBE	AyD
— do —	17th		Batteries registering a few rounds, the ration difficult owing to mist. A.B.C.D. Batteries fired 91 rounds, enemy did not show himself in retaliation. Rounds expended 99.	AyD
— do —	18th	6:54 p.m.	A. Battery was shelled with heavy enemy light field guns for 20 minutes no damage being done. A.B.C. & D. Batteries registered a few enemy batteries found all various ranges in the vicinity of HULLUCH.	

WAR DIARY or INTELLIGENCE SUMMARY

Army Form C. 2118.

70th Bde R.F.A. Divison

Place	Date	Hour	Summary of Events and Information	Remarks and references to Appendices
MAZINGARBE	Oct 18th 1915		Rounds expended 290 Shrapnel H.E.118 Observation difficult owing to rain	H.D.
— do —	19th	11 A.M.	Enemy shelled our Infantry trenches with light Field Guns at intervals during the day. A.B. & D Batteries retaliating on enemy's trenches in the vicinity of BOIS HUGO. At 3.45 P.M. enemy shelled our working party in CHALK PIT WOOD causing five rounds expended by Brigade 273 Shrapnel, 94 H.E.	H.D.
— do —	20th	12.30 P.M.	L Battery attached to 37th HEAVY BRIGADE. 96 do. the duties of Counter Battery at 12.15 P.M. Enemy Field Guns shelled our Infantry trenches in CHALKPIT WOOD. A.B. & D Batteries retaliating on enemy's trenches in BOIS-HUGO. At 4 P.M. A.B. & D Batteries concentrated their fire on BOIS HUGO with 6 rounds of H.E. per gun, doing considerable damage to enemy's trenches. Rounds expended during the day 15-9 Shrapnel 247 H.E.	H.D.
— do —	21st	8 A.M.	Enemy Field Guns shelled our Infantry trenches from the direction of HULLUCH. A.B. & D Batteries retaliating on enemy's communication trenches in the vicinity of BOIS HUGO with good effect. Rounds expended by Brigade during the day 191 Shrapnel, 130 High explosive	H.D.

WAR DIARY
or
INTELLIGENCE SUMMARY.

Army Form C. 2118.

Confidential

(Erase heading not required.)

[Stamp: 70th BRIGADE]

Place	Date	Hour	Summary of Events and Information	Remarks and references to Appendices
MAZINGARBE	Oct 1915 22nd		Enemy's Field Guns shelled our Infantry front line trenches intermittently during the day, R.B. & D. Batteries retaliating on enemy strong points in the vicinity of BOIS. HUGO round expended Shrapnel 40. H.E. 69	N.f.D.
–do–	23rd	10/10 AM	R Battery did 2 rounds on enemy's working party in the vicinity of HULLUCH with good effect. At 2 p.m. enemy shelled our Inf trenches from the direction of HULLUCH. B. Battery retaliated on BOIS. HUGO. & rounds expended by the Brigade 189. Shrapnel 42. H.E. observation nil. during the Night.	N.f.D.
–do–	24th		Enemy's Field Guns shelled our Inf trenches intermittently during the day R.B. & D. Batteries retaliating on enemy's communication trenches in BOIS. HUGO. at 4 p.m. R. B. & D. Batteries concentrated their fire on enemy communicating trench N. of BOIS HUGO with good effect. rounds expended shrapnel 94. H.E. 137.	N.f.D.
–do–	25		Enemy shelled CHALKPIT WOOD, also intermittently during the day. R.B. & D. Batteries retaliating in their communicating trenches at 11 P.M. our batteries concentrated their fire on enemy's strong points in	

1577 Wt.W10791/1773 500,000 1/15 D.D.&L. A.D.S.S./Forms/C. 2118.

70th Bde R.F.A. "April"

WAR DIARY
or
INTELLIGENCE SUMMARY

Army Form C. 2118.

Place	Date	Hour	Summary of Events and Information	Remarks and references to Appendices
MAZINGARBE	October 1915 25th		In the vicinity of BOIS HUGO rounds expended 191 shrapnel. H.E. 44, observation very difficult owing to mist & rain.	YD
— do —	26th	1.50 a.m.	Enemy shelled our Inf front line and support trenches. N. of LOOS with field guns and various shines during the day. A.B. & D. Batteries retaliating on their trenches, rounds expended 48 shrapnel.	YD
— do—	27th		Enemy shelled our Inf trenches intermittently during the day, A.B. & D. Batteries retaliating on enemy trenches, observation difficult owing to rain rounds expended 500 shrapnel	YD
— do —	28th		Enemy shelled our Inf trenches at intervals during the day from the direction of HILL 70. A.B. & D. Batteries retaliating on enemy trenches rounds expended by Brigade 287 shrapnel 241 H.E. Shell	YD
— do—	29th	10. a.m.	Enemy shelled our Inf trenches with light field guns, No. 13 Battery retaliating on their trenches. At 2 p.m. A Battery was heavily shelled with 8 inch armour piercing shell from the direction of CITÉ ST ELIE, destroying one Dug out, rounds expended by Brigade 251 shrapnel 94 H.E.	YD
— do —	30th		Enemy shelled our Inf trenches and LOOS intermittently during the day, at 9a.m. and 11.30 a.m. A Btry was heavily shelled with 8 inch shell, no damage done	YD

WAR DIARY or INTELLIGENCE SUMMARY

Army Form C. 2118.

(Erase heading not required.)

Place	Date	Hour	Summary of Events and Information	Remarks and references to Appendices
MAZINGARBE	October 30th 1915		B & D Batteries retaliating on enemys trenches observation difficult owing to rain & mist. rounds expended by Brigade 59 Shrapnel. 18 y H.E.	JJD
-do-	31st	10 a.m.	Enemy shelled our front line trenches W of HILL 70 at intervals during the day. A. Battery retaliating on enemys trenches. At 2.30 p.m. A.B. & D Batteries counterbatteried their fire on enemys trenches with H.E. shell doing considerable damage. rounds expended by Brigade during the day. 274 Shrapnel. 44 H.E.	JJD

76th Bde: RFA.
Vol: 3

15th Division

121/7656

Nov 15

Confidential.

Army Form C. 2118.

70th BRIGADE R.F.A.

40th Bde. R.F.A.

WAR DIARY
or
INTELLIGENCE SUMMARY.

(Erase heading not required.)

Instructions regarding War Diaries and Intelligence Summaries are contained in F.S. Regs., Part II. and the Staff Manual respectively. Title pages will be prepared in manuscript.

Place	Date	Hour	Summary of Events and Information	Remarks and references to Appendices
Fricourt	1/11/15		Enemy shewed our front-line trencher with light field guns & 5"9" Howitzers. We retaliated on enemy trenches in Sct. Sec A. & A.11. Effect good. Fire lightly shewed Bty.	
"	2/11/15		Enemy shewed our front-line communication trenches lightly. We retaliated in usual with instructions from 4yth D.A. German heavy Howt. dealt by Flacker N 98° from 7.29.b.1.9.	B²
	3/11/15		Enemy shewed Blockist Wood & trenches with 4"2" howitzers & fired with heavy. We retaliated.	B²
	4/11/15		Enemy shewed our front-line trenches & heavy howitzers. We retaliated by near of 4yth D.A.	B²
	5/11/15		Our trenches heavily shelled, our retaliation was very heavy with good effect.	B² B²
	6/11/15		Our trenches shewed intermittently during the day. retaliation by order of 4yth D.A. during the afternoon our Fire & Support trenches shewed by light field guns & 5"9" howitzer & black Gd wood by 5"9" & 8" how. Retaliation by order of 4yth D.A.	
	7/11/15		Our "A" battery shewed shewed during the afternoon, also Blackput Wood & communication trenches behind hour. Retaliated with good effect.	B² B²

1577 Wt.W10791/1773 500,000 1/15 D.D.&L. A.D.S.S./Forms/C. 2118.

WAR DIARY or INTELLIGENCE SUMMARY

Army Form C. 2118.

70th Bde. R.F.A.

Place	Date	Hour	Summary of Events and Information	Remarks and references to Appendices
Hooge	9/11/15		Our forward trenches were shelled at intervals, however, during the day. Retaliated on enemy front line for ammunition trenches. Short bombardment of enemy spots by order of 47th D.A. Retaliation by enemy light.	R.
	10/11/15		Chequerboard, our ammunition trenches, Hooge & our "A" battery observed during the day. Retaliation on enemy front line support trenches & by order of 47th D.A. performed good effect.	R.
	11/11/15		Our front line trenches & Hooge however shelled. We retaliated on enemy front line support trenches.	R.
	12/11/15		Chequerboard, Hooge & trenches in Section A.1. shelled lightly. We retaliated effectively.	R.
	13/11/15		In retaliation to bombardment on "Wood 3" enemy shelled Section A.1. very heavily. A few shells thrown into Hooge. We retaliated at request of Infantry regiment by order of 47th D.A.	R.
	14/11/15		Trenches shelled during the day, we retaliated together at request of Infantry also by order of 47th D.A.	R.
	15/11/15		At intervals of half an hour, commencing at 3 p.m., the looking section of each	R.

70th Bde. R.F.A. WAR DIARY or INTELLIGENCE SUMMARY

Army Form C. 2118.

Place	Date	Hour	Summary of Events and Information	Remarks and references to Appendices
Mazingarbe	15/10/15		Battery "A.B.C & D"/70th Bde R.F.A. pulled out of their respective gun pits to make room for moving section of 1st Div Arty. One section proceeded to Vermelles & have they relieved corresponding section of batteries of 91st Bde. Section reported on relief in new position G14a (Trench Map "Provisional Series N° 3 1/10,000. + Brigade in line.	
	16/10/15		Relieving section in new position effected necessary improvements to pits + proceeded with registrations. Rear section of batteries pulled out of pits, being relieved by new sections of 1st D.A. at ~3 p.m. + proceeded to relieve corresponding section of 91st Bde. All guns reported in action & in position by hour at 8 p.m.	
	17/10/15		Short bombardments on portions relieved by 15th D.A. + registrations carried out. Enemy retaliated weakly.	
	18/10/15		Batteries continued registering, + carried out shortbombardments as arranged by 15th D.A. Enemy retaliated weaker.	
	19/10/15		Observation difficult owing to mist. Enemy shelled our supporting trenches in Sub-Section C II lightly during the day with light field guns.	

70th Bde. R.F.A.

WAR DIARY or INTELLIGENCE SUMMARY.

Army Form C. 2118.

Place	Date	Hour	Summary of Events and Information	Remarks and references to Appendices
Mazingarbe	21/11/15		Heavy cal. short bombardment of trenches executed by 15th D.A. Enemy retaliated on "A"/70. "A" Battery engaged in knocking out a machine gun emplacement during the afternoon. Considerable damage effected.	A
	22/11/15		Further slow bombardment carried out by order of D.A. Enemy retaliated on our front line & support trenches lightly.	A
	22/11/15		"A" Battery again engaged on machine gun emplacement. Shell was purely destructive. Enemy fired a few rounds with trench mortars at LA BASSÉE with HE. At 5pm one section of A.B C&D Batteries replied in two positions, namely "B"/62nd Bde & "C"/62nd Bde, under orders to retire in one hrs. time at 4.30pm.	A
	23/11/15		Owing to heavy mist, impossible to ascertain with certainty at new positions. During the evening new sections of A, B, C, D Batteries moved into new positions & old guns reported in action on emphones by 4.30 pm.	A
Vermelles	24/11/15		Batteries adjusted gun pits required. At 10 am Dis. Bois taken over from the 12th Div. by the 15th Div. In retaliation for our registering, enemy shelled our front line & support trenches Bryans Zone from.	A

70th Bde. R.F.A. WAR DIARY or INTELLIGENCE SUMMARY.

Army Form C. 2118.

Place	Date	Hour	Summary of Events and Information	Remarks and references to Appendices
Vermelles	24/10/15 25/10/15		from G6 d 94 to G5 a 23. On our right 1st Div. on our left 2nd Div. Enemy shelled our front line trenches & support trenches with light & heavy field guns in the morning. Our own 18 pounders with light & heavy field howitzers. Retaliation with good effect.	R.
	26/10/15		Of 12 rounds C.H.E fired by an enemy light field howitzer, between 2.20pm & 2.45pm on our front line trenches 4 rounds were blind. Retaliation fire opened and registering.	R.
	27/10/15		Enemy artillery busy all day in shelling our front line communication trenches. We retaliated & also carried out frequent searches for enemy batteries. Registering by our batteries continued.	R.
	28/10/15		Our front line trenches shelled with light field gun at intervals during the day. We retaliated & carried out searches by mean of 18 pd Q.F.	R.
	29/10/15		Enemy shelled our front line trenches during the am. with light field gun. We retaliation on enemy front line communication trenches, also carried out registration by aid of F.O.A.	R.
	30/10/15		Enemy shelled our trenches with the howitz. until light was gone. Our batteries retaliated. Each battery registered several points.	R.

To the Pres: BTA.
vol. 4

12/7935.

15th V

WAR DIARY or INTELLIGENCE SUMMARY

Army Form C. 2118.

10th B.de R.F.A.

Place	Date	Hour	Summary of Events and Information	Remarks and references to Appendices
Vermelles	1/12/15		Enemy shelled our trenches at intervals during the day with light shell. Great retaliation on German trenches. Supported by "A" & "C" also carried out slow bombardment by order of D.A.	B.
	2/12/15		Germans our papers not supported by "B" battery, ricochets damage being done to the parapet. Enemy shelled our trenches with rifle grenades from G. [illegible]	B.
	3/12/15		Trenches. Retaliation with effect. Machine gun emplacement fire bombarded by "B" battery which went slight retaliation by the enemy. Specified bombardment carried out by order of D.A. Enemy retaliation very slight.	B.
	4/12/15		Our situation heavily shelled by enemy light field guns we retaliated by means of [illegible]. No casualties.	B.
	5/12/15	11 am	Enemy airplane bombs dropped on our trenches with field guns 4.2" & 5.9" howitzers. The battery [illegible] till the bombardment was the heavy on our communication trenches. The howitzer battery for about an hour retaliated heavily. Our bombardment [illegible] during the day appeared to be very effective.	B.
	6/12/15		Our trenches shelled at intervals during the day. We retaliated with effect.	B.

WAR DIARY 70th Bde. R.F.A.
INTELLIGENCE SUMMARY

Army Form C. 2118.

(Erase heading not required.)

Place	Date	Hour	Summary of Events and Information	Remarks and references to Appendices
Vermelles	6/12/15		A few HE shells fell near our "A" & "C" batteries, no damage being done. Roof of no. 2 hut gun emplacement knocked off by "A" battery.	R.
	7/12/15		Our trenches shelled lightly during the morning, but during the afternoon following our bombardment at 2-2.15 pm the enemy retaliated heavily with 4.2", 5.9". "A"/70 silenced enemy battery.	R.
	8/12/15		Bombardment by "A"/70 on enemy working parties very effective. C/70 considerably damaged a working line emplacement. A few rounds repulsed by batteries.	R.
	9/12/15		Enemy retaliated very heavily & his own bombardment at 1.30 pm. Demolished 2 of the enemy five sences at 1 pm.	R.
	10/12/15		Enemy trench was found partienles during the day with light field guns, but retaliated. "A" "B" "D" batteries did considerable damage to enemy machine gun emplacements & their trenches during the day.	R.
	11/12/15		Arial hostile shell struck our Gripner Posn & makes gun emplacements by "A" & "B" batteries & their being thrown out, the air on each case. Our "A" & "C" batteries also silenced during the afternoon by 4.2", 5.9" & 8". No damage was done. VERMELLES shelled with guns of narrow calibre.	R.

40th Bde. R.F.A. WAR DIARY or INTELLIGENCE SUMMARY

Army Form C. 2118.

Place	Date	Hour	Summary of Events and Information	Remarks and references to Appendices
Vermelles	12/9/15		Enemy shelled our trenches at intervals during the day, & ranged our heavy howitzers on our front line, stopping him at 2.30 pm with lght. field guns to 4.2". "B" & "D" batteries carried out bombardments of enemy working parties in front line trenches & strong points. We practised hourly fire on enemy chinney. We carried out charn-bombardment by order of D.A. during the day, the enemy retaliated by shelling our trenches with lght. field guns, fuse-nosed shrapnel & retaliation. "A" Battery chased enemy working gun reinforcement, causing considerable damage.	R
	13/9/15		Enemy shelled our trenches with lght. field guns & 4.2" Sepetrebrich. "D" Battery engaged enemy working gun emplacements & did extensive damage to parapet.	C
	14/9/15		Enemy shelled our trenches at various times during the day with lght. field guns & heavy row ones moving in Q.8.a with 5.9". One section of Lewen Burgess at 3pm.	R
	15/9/15		Battery was relieved by sections of 5th Levern Burgess at 3pm.	R
	16/9/15		Enemy shelled our trenches slightly several times during the day with lght. field guns & reliables. Rear section of 'C' battery relieved by 'B'.	R

1577 Wt.W10791/1773 500,000 1/15 D.D. & L. A.D.S.S./Forms/C. 2118.

Army Form C. 2118.

40th B". WAR DIARY R.F.A.

or

INTELLIGENCE SUMMARY.

(Erase heading not required.)

Instructions regarding War Diaries and Intelligence Summaries are contained in F. S. Regs., Part II. and the Staff Manual respectively. Title pages will be prepared in manuscript.

Place	Date	Hour	Summary of Events and Information	Remarks and references to Appendices
Vermelles	16/9/15		Two Sections of 5th Howr. Bugade at 5.30pm. arrived here & turned over the personnel of am Bon to the 5th Howr Bugade with Divl. Arty. The 3rd. Bugade (40th) marched back to rest and were in rest at the house in fields.	
Marles-les-Mines	17/9/15		40th Bde being put into rest. Hun Genl. to turn, to Clean Workshops & dry clothing, harnesses etc "A" Battery Brigade requested to	
	18/9/15		have cleaning, greasing gun drill etc. general routine.	
	19/9/15		Recruit gun workshop cleaning, drill usual work, the Brigade became General routine.	
	20/9/15		Orders taken for tests march by the Bde. Comdr. Brig R. Bratowe inspected in stables gun detail etc.	
	21/10/15		Signalling horses harnesses also Batteries by B. B's & Bde. Brig Dr.	
	22/10/15		Horses stables & drill general and by Brig Dr.	
	23/10/15		"A" & "B" Batteries did a route march "B D" & Bde Column worked	
	24/9/15		out proved drill. 40th Battery arrived out a route march.	

1577 Wt.W10791/1773 500,000 1/15 D. D. & L. A.D.S.S./Forms/C. 2118.

Army Form C. 2118.

70th Bde. R.F.A.

WAR DIARY
or
INTELLIGENCE SUMMARY.
(Erase heading not required.)

Instructions regarding War Diaries and Intelligence Summaries are contained in F. S. Regs., Part II. and the Staff Manual respectively. Title pages will be prepared in manuscript.

Place	Date	Hour	Summary of Events and Information	Remarks and references to Appendices
Mater-fer- Aines	25/12/15		Observed & holiday. Reserve & 113th Co. ting carried out as usual.	R
	26/12/15		Reserve duties.	R
	27/11/12/15		Reserve, 113th Co. & gun drill.	R
	28/12/15		Bde. 113th taken for route march by Brigade Commander. Batteries engaged in gun, machining & training duties.	R
	29/12/15		Brigade Commander engaged in examining Bru. subalterns in gun drill. Gun mechanism, laying out lines of fire, running the memory, to fuses & magnt Sending the aft fuses.	R
	30/12/15		Subalterns taken out by Bde. Commander for examination in recon. reiture &c. in the direction of Batton, Fontaine & OP's.	R
	31/12/15		Brigade List paid in. Divisional fielding fetters. Service stables & drills carried out by Batteries & rout march by Bde. Commn.	R

W W A Christie
Lt-Col
Comdg 70 Brigade R.F.A.

70th Bay R.F.A.
Vol. 5-

Jan' 16

15

WAR DIARY or INTELLIGENCE SUMMARY

Army Form C. 2118

70th Bde R.F.A.

(Erase heading not required.)

Instructions regarding War Diaries and Intelligence Summaries are contained in F. S. Regs, Part II. and the Staff Manual respectively. Title Pages will be prepared in manuscript.

Place	Date	Hour	Summary of Events and Information	Remarks and references to Appendices
Marles-le-Mines	1/1/16	—	Batteries - knee layers signaling & telephones - Bde. Colm word work & drill orders. Inspection by Bde. Commdr.	
	2/1/16	—	Bdes. Colm stores. Relieved by 4th Dragoons of pres. bil.	
	3/1/16		Bdes. Colm. stores.	
	4/1/16		Drawing Harness, saving gun drill & laying etc.	
	5/1/16		Routine. The Brigade participated in Divisional Scheme. Batteries at La Turnel for the night.	
Estruval	6/1/16		Divisional Scheme continued - "B"/70th Bde. forming part of Advance Guard. Returned to La Turnel & billeted for the night.	
	7/1/16		Divisional Scheme concluded & Bde. returned to Barracks at Barless. Res. horses.	
Marles-les-Mines	8/1/16		Gun Drill laying etc. of the Brigade proceeded to Barrens to take a Course in Telephony etc. Batteries & Columns engaged in carrying out the ordinary work.	
	9/1/16		Routine. Ran extra telephony Signaling & testing searching drill. Lectures delivered from Divisional Cables delivered by Brigade Commander with the Officers of the Brigade. Inspection by Divisional General - Maj. Gen. MacCracken.	
	10/1/16		Returning general Routine work.	
	11/1/16			
	12/1/16		Returning horses, harness, general stores.	
	13/1/16		General parade with inspection by Brigade Commander.	
	14/1/16		Preparing to return next billets.	

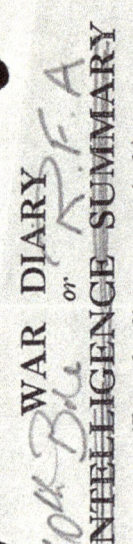

WAR DIARY or INTELLIGENCE SUMMARY

Army Form C. 2118

70th Bde R.F.A.

Place	Date	Hour	Summary of Events and Information	Remarks and references to Appendices
Martes-les-Mines	14/9/16		A section of each Battery forwarded its waggons following this return of the 54th Battery & D/176 Battery & Section of "C" Battery plus a section of the relieved portion of the 115th Battery, the section of "A" Battery going into the relieved portion at Philosophe.	P/1
Mazingarbe	18/9/16		Registration carried out by section in return. Rammy Battalion of "A", "B", "C", "D" Batteries came into action during the evening. Baggot Zone registration taken over by Brigade Commander. Enemy heavy trench mortar & rifle grenade fire.	P/1
	19/9/16		Batteries carried out previously registration. Hostile strafing light.	P/1
	15/9/16		Enemy shelled our front line trenches with light field guns 4.13's & 5.9's during the day. Its batteries were registered from registered reval points.	P/1
	19/9/16		Batteries continued registering. Enemy batteries on ... with all calibre guns during the day. "D" batteries O.P. also shelled.	P/1
	20/9/16		Batteries retaliated for any shewing of our trenches.	P/1
	21/9/16		"A" Battery shelled working party at Puits 13 Bis. Enemy retired to fire his ammunition trenches. No retaliation with ...	P/1
	22/9/16		Enemy shelled our trenches, Brick pit, road & trolley. No retaliation. We also fired by request of infantry.	P/1
	23/9/16		Enemy trench mortars very active. Enemy shelled our trenches with light field guns 9 - 5.9's during the day.	P/1
	24/9/16		Enemy placed Battalion in 4.26 x 24 will column of two three rounds (probably Major 36c NW). Enemy guns active on our trenches, the retaliation.	P/1
	25/9/16		Enemy guns very active on Chalk pit road, Chalk pit & other trenches during the day. No retaliation.	P/1
	26/9/16		They also shelled our trenches in enemy by night. During the day the enemy shelled our trenches heavily with high field guns 4.13's & 5.9's. No retaliation.	P/1

WAR DIARY or INTELLIGENCE SUMMARY

70th Bde R.F.A.

Army Form C. 2118

Place	Date	Hour	Summary of Events and Information	Remarks and references to Appendices
Mazingarbe	24/1/16		The enemy shelled our trenches very heavy during the day, causing us good damage. We retaliated heavily shelling 5th German attacked over the line severed by "A" & "C" batteries 70th Bde. Also in the line of the enemy barrage opened by their batteries. No enemy machine rifle fire. The attack broke down.	B
	28/1/16		Enemy shelled Chalk-Pit Wood very heavily during the afternoon with all calibre guns. We retaliated heavily. The Brigade carried out Bombardment as arranged by 13th D.A. Three howitzers caused little retaliation at intervals during the day. Its enemy shelled two trenches of Chalk Pit Wood but was heavy. Our 8" Howitzers carried out a bombardment of enemy trenches during the afternoon. The 70th Bde Batteries were very silent helping to subdue movement by its enemy. Nothing however transpired to harass them firing.	B B B
	29/1/16		Very foggy - very quiet	B
	30/1/16			
	31/1/16		Enemy shelled our front line trenches during the day with high field guns & H 13; They also appeared to be registering our trenches in Sq 24 d J. G 23 & H 19 with H 13: H 19s Howitzers (my Trench Map 36cNW) Hill 70 & L.00s were bombarded during the afternoon. Enemy airman to be very busy logging all along the Brigade front. Batteries activities in enemy trenches. The undermentioned officers were mentioned in Dispatches early this month. A/Lt-Col. W.A.Christie. C.M.G. Bde Commander. No 61 Sgt. O.S.M. Franklin S.G. "A/70"Bde. No 85/152 Cpl. T. Rees "A/40" Bde. No 36682 Gr. A.W. Tucker B/y Sgnlt. "B/70" and this month No 90299 Lc B. Revell. "B/70" and Bde were awarded the D.C.M.	B

MWQ Christie

R Ward
Comdy 70th Brigade RFA

Army Form C. 2118

WAR DIARY or INTELLIGENCE SUMMARY

70th Bde. R.F.A.

(Erase heading not required.)

Instructions regarding War Diaries and Intelligence Summaries are contained in F. S. Regs., Part II. and the Staff Manual respectively. Title Pages will be prepared in manuscript.

Place	Date	Hour	Summary of Events and Information	Remarks and references to Appendices
Mazingarbe	1/2/16		Enemy shelled our front line trenches slightly at intervals during the day. The batteries at 1-40a.m. & were shelled at 8 & 10.30 pm with light field howitzers. No damage was done. Hun supervision in HULLUCH apparently no ammunition supply blown up.	A.
	2/2/16		Enemy heavy arm Super between H.25.b. centred y. H.19.d.23 (of trench Map 36cNW 3) on our front line trenches was shelled slightly with light field guns or similar during 10-10a. Retaliation effective.	A.
	3/2/16.		"B"/70 fired in Super neavy enrolments damage. Enemy felt with no new front bn with H.2.i. LOOS shelled during the morning. Enemy howitzers HILL 40. At 5.15pm enemy opened a new at Bere of LOOS Graves. Our batteries were not effective retaliation.	C.
	4/2/16		Our trenches were shelled slightly during the day. Batteries presumed wooden from rest at H.25.d.34 was subsequent by "B"/70. "D"/70 engage new trayer Machinegun emplacements at H.25.d.03 & H.25.d.9.87. (of trench Map 36bNW 3)	R.
	5/2/16.		Barrditive normal. Batter fining with light fuses form our trenches during the day "C"/70 fined in PUTTS 13 broo. recognized new dugout probably an O.P. St. heads & H.25.b. reported up & shots fired. Between other were fired.	R.R.
	6/2/16		Our trenches slightly or without damage.	R.R.
	7/2/16		Enemy activity in ordin loses. No returns effectively.	B.
	8/2/16.		"C"/70 heavily shelled by 5-9's from 11am to 12.30pm than 2.15pm to 2.30 pm. About 100 rounds were fired. No 1 Gun pit our of action. Runfuly considered damaged. Enemy shelled our trenches heavily with light field guns & howitzers at intervals during the day. They also shelled batteries at MASSY with 5-9's.	B.

1875 Wt. W 593/826 1,000,000 4/15 J.B.C. & A. A.D.S.S./Forms/C. 2118.

Army Form C. 2118

WAR DIARY or INTELLIGENCE SUMMARY

40th B.de R.F.A.

(Erase heading not required.)

Instructions regarding War Diaries and Intelligence Summaries are contained in F. S. Regs., Part II. and the Staff Manual respectively. Title Pages will be prepared in manuscript.

Place	Date	Hour	Summary of Events and Information	Remarks and references to Appendices
Mazingarbe	9/2/16		A German showing partly mangled [?] was observed on the enemy front line during the afternoon. D/40 intermittently opened fire & obtained direct hits. Enemy were shelled slightly during the day.	P.S.
	10/2/16		Enemy shelled our trenches with H.25.b.4.9. 0. H.25.b.4.5. a. 5.9's at intervals during the day. Sap heads from H.25.b.4.9. 0. H.25.b.4.5. are being constructed up, wire has been erected in front of this new trench.	P.S.
	11/2/16		During the day enemy bombarded our trenches with hy. fuzed guns H.25 a 5.9. between 5.15pm & 5.40pm fired guns/light howitzer shells on trenches opposite HULLUCH intervals. he rapidity of fire being about 40 rounds per minute. He returned frequently.	P.S.
	12/2/16		Enemy again bombarded our front line & supported trenches very heavily between 3.8pm 3.40pm his hy. fuzed guns & howitzers fired at the rate of about 50 rounds per minute. D.C. Retaliated.	P.S.
	13/2/16		Batteries at H.19.d.1.6 were sniped by "A"/40. Enemy shelled our front line trenches - Breslau Road at intervals during the day.	P.S.
	14/2/16		Enemy shelled our trenches & intervals during the day. He retaliated. Normal.	P.S.
	15/2/16		New war[?] by trenches reported by "A"/40. B/40 opened on new work in H.25.b. D/40 sniped trenches & repaired. Enemy shelled our trenches slightly during the day.	P.S.
	16/2/16		Hostile artillery very quiet today.	P.S.
	19/2/16		Enemy shelled our trenches during the day with hy. fuzed guns. His fire was effective. Normal sniper his own trenches & front line [?]. He became again in front of enemy front line. B/40 served on by D/40 on similar to [?] enemy front line. B/40 served on [?] hostile attack with trench mortars at 4.30pm team.	P.S.

Army Form C. 2118

WAR DIARY or INTELLIGENCE SUMMARY

70th Bde: R.F.A.

(Erase heading not required.)

Instructions regarding War Diaries and Intelligence Summaries are contained in F.S. Regs., Part II. and the Staff Manual respectively. Title Pages will be prepared in manuscript.

Place	Date	Hour	Summary of Events and Information	Remarks and references to Appendices
Mazingarbe	18/2/16		Enemy shelled our front line trenches very heavily from 'D'/70 upper front on Rhubarb to front of enemy trench, Vickers Mary hill also rifleing of the Coburlion trench light, also the recent on Rap Berry 6.1 from R/R the Koens trenches	R/-
	19/2/16		Hostile artillery active on trenches anywhere between Rays, and bridge, field guns 'B'/70 carried out retaliation on Rayon trench & Vickers trench.	R/-
	20/2/16		'A'/70 were active this morning with 5.9"s. A percent of enemy trenches was shelled with 5.9"s to hinder the position field guns & also caused 'D'/70 to engage them. Their nights 'D'/70 also engaged hostile machine guns emplacements 'A'/70 also engaged hostile machine gun emplacement. Our trenches were shelled very lightly last night. Field guns fired today.	R/-
	21/2/16		Trench mortars & Singles in Rathlin were active in intervals. Enemy shelled our trenches with 5.9"s & 2"s. Enemy renewed front at 9.30 am & about 2 rounds per minute until 1 pm. No damage was done. Hi div. 'B'/70 or 'D'/70. During the night field guns emptied their guns next of force of much sharp of events than usual.	R/-
	22/2/16		Enemy trench mortars continued during the day, and eight of fire guns in 2's. De rationed an Rincon trenches. Approx. of no stray fired cannot see the amount ascertained. During the night. 'D'/70 were cleared the trenches and 1 light guns was initiated 10.30 p.m. until 5.9"s in light	R/-
	23/2/16		again this day, also some of the same 'D'/70. Enemy canned more fire lights this night in lieu of them.	R/-
	24/2/16		Nightly shewing of trenches by enemy light trench guns 'C'/70 allied by 15cm Balance 2.30pm - 3.40pm to damage.	R/-

WAR DIARY or INTELLIGENCE SUMMARY

70th Bde T.A.

Army Form C. 2118

(Erase heading not required.)

Place	Date	Hour	Summary of Events and Information	Remarks and references to Appendices
Meteren	25/2/16		Hostile artillery active on kinks intermittently during the day. "D"/70 were shelled by heavy trench howitzers from 4.30pm to 9pm, damage was done.	P.C.
	26/2/16		"A"/70 received visit kits on firing point. No damage. "D"/70 again shelled by light howitzer. Killed H 26 c + G 30 d fort 3.35 pm. Dispersed enemy with m.g. & rifle. Retaliated with airgun.	P.C.
	27/2/16		Several of our trenches by enemy artillery fairly slight. Our batteries delivering effective fire. Shelled ration parties. Enemy trenches seriously damaged in WINGLES.	P.C.
	28/2/16		Hostile trench mortars shelled our trenches heavily from H 25 L central. "B"/70 retaliated & silenced enemy trench mortar. "A"/70 engaged enemy cup head X8 also Bridge at H 20 d y 8 h, & silenced enemy. Fire at H 20 L b 4 (ref Trench Map 36 c NW)	P.C.
	29/2/16		"A"/70 obtained 22 direct hits on enemy O.P. & wire. Hostile artillery especially howitzers have shown activity during the last few days. Enemy shelled our trenches slightly during the forenoon. Enemy shelling from 10.45am to 11.45am & knocked out our artillery observation station who managed to avoid casualties. Enemy trench mortars very active this morning but the high.	P.C.

W.H. Clark
Lt-Col
Comdg 70 Brigade R.F.A.

Army Form C. 2118

WAR DIARY
70th Bde or R.T.A.
INTELLIGENCE SUMMARY
(Erase heading not required.)

Instructions regarding War Diaries and Intelligence Summaries are contained in F.S. Regs., Part II. and the Staff Manual respectively. Title Pages will be prepared in manuscript.

Place	Date	Hour	Summary of Events and Information	Remarks and references to Appendices
Mazingabe 1916	1/3/16	—	Enemy artillery shewed some increase slightly above normal during the day but fairly quiet. De intensiv artillery efficer on our frontiers. A/40 Bot twelve shells bursting on Keep at H 20 a & 8 Thirteen 4/10,000 Battn 6. 36 a.w.f. Active gun at PITS in B." shewed by D/40. Slight shewing of our trenches by H.E. A 21. fired from an unidentifies Day Bombardment of an unknown Strong point at H 20 6.2.9. Several guns experienced in it. H 31 c. 4.h 8h engaged unreliable damage done. Hostile artillery very quiet. Several Targets engaged by Batteries with good effect.	
	3/3/16	—		
	4/3/16	—	Reserve.	
	5/3/16	—		
	6/3/16	—	Enemy artillery heavy and full actions very quiet. Fired rapidly and engaged with shrapnel. Enemy batteries active. Hostile artillery now active— our trenches shelled slightly without much damage. Field guns & howitzers + several Saps Mound Expansion engaged & answered by Batteries.	
	7/3/16	—	Normal light shewing of our trenches the enemy artillery were ad howitzers retaliation t rating. Several trenches to town between ours & Howitzer's Scratched Practice wire destroyed by D/40 Howitzers. The D heavy batteries H 21. 6 5.5. burnt trenches ? Sunde Bridges engaged Today between different.	
	9/3/16	—	Hostile artillery increased action. Enemy Observation Stations engaged by our Batteries. Battalion H.P.'s rations points engaged by our Batteries with effect. Enemy batteries after attempts intensely active. Anotherwise shelled shrapnel. A/40 4/2+ fired three rounds 9 Lens, our trenches detached Batteries & continued damage we by many fight & field gun Observations. Enemy artillery action increased by night Batteries.	
	10/3/16	—		
	11/3/16	—		
	13/3/16	—	Enemy artillery action normal. Two hostile heavy guns (5'9") exchanged shell. H.29 d.5.2 shells the N. front of the Double Crassier fired 30 shots to N.W. about 150 rounds. were fired off which about 100 were shell.	

1875 Wt. W593/826 1,000,000 4/15 J.B.C. & A. A.D.S.S./Forms/C. 2118.

Confidential

Instructions regarding War Diaries and Intelligence Summaries are contained in F. S. Regs., Part II. and the Staff Manual respectively. Title Pages will be prepared in manuscript.

WAR DIARY or ~~INTELLIGENCE SUMMARY~~

70th Bde R.F.A.

(Erase heading not required.)

Army Form C. 2118

Place	Date 1916	Hour	Summary of Events and Information	Remarks and references to Appendices
Mazingarbe	14/3/16		Our trenches shelled during the day with light field guns, 4.2"s & 5.9" Hows. Rather above normal. We retaliated effectively on each occasion. Batteries at FOSSE 7 shelled heavily from BOIS-de-DIXHUIT & LENS. Various targets engaged by our batteries with effect.	
	15/3/16		Hostile shelling normal.	
	16/3/16		Hostile artillery more active. Our trenches were shelled at frequent intervals during the day. Working parties dispersed by our batteries & suspected O.P's, registering points & machine gun emplacements engaged.	
	17/3/16		Enemy artillery were very active today & shelled our trenches heavily at frequent intervals with light & heavy guns & Howitzers.	
	18/3/16		Enemy artillery again active, but limited supply of ammunition prevented really effective retaliation. Considerable work is now being done in hostile lines.	
	19/3/16		Red paper balloon dropped on A/70 by Enemy plane, this morning but no shelling of position followed. Our trenches have been shelled lightly today with light field guns & 4.2's & Chalkpit Wood rather heavily with light & heavy guns & howitzers.	
	20/3/16		Much work is being carried out in the Enemy lines. Hostile shelling normal.	
	21/3/16		Our trenches have been shelled lightly today with light field guns.	
	22/3/16		Some new work observed in Enemy lines. Shelling normal.	
	23/3/16		Machine gun emplacement engaged & considerably damaged by D/70. Artillery on both sides quiet.	
	24/3/16		Normal.	
	25/3/16		Suspected O.P. engaged & materially damaged by A/70. Enemy shelled our trenches slightly at intervals.	

1875 Wt. W593/826 1,000,000 4/15 J.B.C. & A. A.D.S.S./Forms/C. 2118.

Confidential

Army Form C. 2118

WAR DIARY
or
INTELLIGENCE SUMMARY
10th Bde RFA
(Erase heading not required.)

Instructions regarding War Diaries and Intelligence Summaries are contained in F.S. Regs., Part II. and the Staff Manual respectively. Title Pages will be prepared in manuscript.

Place	Date 1916	Hour	Summary of Events and Information	Remarks and references to Appendices
Mazingarbe	26/3/16	—	Enemy exploded small mine opposite VENDIN ALLEY. Bombarded new front line trenches at H19c & H19a west at 4.15 & 5.9 pm. Work at Bamage & M40 suspended during the day. No registrations were observed. Two rounds fired into front line by battery seventy rounds into their line.	JR
	27/3/16		Registration duties on hostile batteries. Movement, suspicious objects registration normal. No activity.	JR
	28/3/16		Registration duties on junction of POSEN ALLEY & GUN TRENCH and on hostile battery F on sharts.	JR
	29/3/16		Hostile battery activities two rounds replied shot by our battery retaliation.	JR
	30/3/16		Enemy activities normal active.	JR
	31/3/16		Hostile artillery shelled our trenches slightly during the day. D/40 dispersed enemy working party at H32 a 5b. (Ref Trench Map 1/10,000 Sheet 36c N.W.) Sheet 6.	JR

WSH Unwin
Lt. Col.
Commd 10th Bde R.F.A.

Confidential

Instructions regarding War Diaries and Intelligence Summaries are contained in F. S. Regs., Part II. and the Staff Manual respectively. Title pages will be prepared in manuscript.

WAR DIARY or INTELLIGENCE SUMMARY.

70th Bde R.F.A.

XV

(Erase heading not required.)

Army Form C. 2118.

70 R F A
Vol 8

Place	Date	Hour	Summary of Events and Information	Remarks and references to Appendices
Mazingarbe	1/4/16		Enemy shelled our trenches at intervals during the day. Hostile [illegible] gun emplacements & registering points engaged effectively.	[illegible]
	2/4/16		Enemy energetically employed on saps. Retaliating, repeated our shelling of working parties very effective. Hostile Artillery normally active.	[illegible]
	3/4/16		Hostile shelling of our trenches normal, retaliation effective. Enemy exposed a [illegible] on [illegible] Front: our artillery active until infantry satisfied with position. M.G. emplacement engaged, but no [illegible] [illegible] to be this [illegible] built for field gun to put out of action.	[illegible]
	4/4/16		Further work reported on enemy saps notwithstanding harassing activity of my brigade. Hostile shelling normal.	[illegible]
	5/4/16		Enemy artillery & trench mortars active against our trenches. Germans [illegible] heavily engaged on new saps & communication trenches. [illegible] post engaged but no material damage done as [illegible] [illegible].	[illegible]
	6/4/16		Our trenches heavily shelled during the day with 4.2", 5.9" & light field guns. We retaliated.	[illegible]

1577 Wt. W10791/1773 500,000 1/15 D. D. & L. A.D.S.S./Forms/C. 2118.

Confidential

1/8th Bn DYA

Army Form C. 2118.

WAR DIARY
or
INTELLIGENCE SUMMARY.

(Erase heading not required.)

Instructions regarding War Diaries and Intelligence Summaries are contained in F. S. Regs., Part II. and the Staff Manual respectively. Title pages will be prepared in manuscript.

Place	Date	Hour	Summary of Events and Information	Remarks and references to Appendices
Maxim goole	1/7/16		Duel H.E. & shrap. on enemy O.P. and stamp L. front. B/D at work all night preparing for battle shelling of our trenches	
	8/7/16		Enemy shelled our trenches intermittently during the day & night. We did not reply effectively on enemy front lines. The power house and our strong pts. on enemy support trenches by [illeg] lines.	
	9/7/16		Our trenches again shelled intermittently such as 2.& 5.9" shrapnel. But not very [illeg].	
	10/7/16		Had our guns shelled active & frequently engaged & returned by D/A. Trenches shelling not very intense. Our artillery Reg/tll not of good effect.	
	11/7/16		Hostile Artillery shelled our trenches during the day - our retaliation proved effective. Little movement observed behind enemy lines.	
	12/7/16 13/7/16		Enemy Artillery noticeably active. Trees removed at WIMBLE's observed B/A Division relieved	
	14/7/16		Reapers posnt engaged damaged. Enemy shewn no tendency at [illeg]	

Confidential

WAR DIARY or INTELLIGENCE SUMMARY
Army Form C. 2118

4th Bde RHA

Place	Date	Hour	Summary of Events and Information	Remarks and references to Appendices
Mazingarbe	14/4/16		Animals during the day. Situation with no good effect.	
	15/4/16		Enemy artillery action somewhat slacker during the day by hostile batteries.	
	16/4/16		Batteries received new registration by aeroplane observation. At 4pm Brigade Zone handed over to the responsibility of Lt Col Thom, Commanding 174th Brigade RFA by Brigade orders. New units under GHQ Reserve at Ecquedecques.	
Ecquedecques	17/4/16		Naval matter of situation. Relieving guns will oppose it.	
	18/4/16		Instruction in ranging bicarbonate; general Aukeery went for gunnery/ammunition officers by Brigade Commander. Two patterns received and [illegible] 28/4/16.	
	28/4/16		Relief picture of "A/40" "B/40" "C/40" movements previous this morning at Vermelles. "A/40" returned "A/63" "B/40" to "C/40" coming under the command of the Left Group.	
Vermelles	29/4/16		Remaining picture movements were made midnight. D/40 remaining at Ecquedecques for training purposes. Command of Right Group & responsibilities of Right Group from taken over by Lt Col Hugh Christie CMG Right Group consisting of "A/40". A. B. C. & D/42 & D/43 with Section of C/43.	
	30/4/16		Enemy Artillery very active, shelling our trench support lines, which 4.25 5"Q's 6"pdrs guns by retaliation obtained served our supporting dividing "A" & "C/40" and utilized for Counter Battery work from 16/4/16 to 28/4/16.	

W H Smith
1. Und

SECRET

WAR DIARY
40th Bde: or R.F.A.
INTELLIGENCE SUMMARY

Army Form C. 2118.

Place	Date	Hour	Summary of Events and Information	Remarks and references to Appendices
Philosophe	1/5/16		Hostile artillery energetic throughout the day on our trenches in G.11, G.10, G.11 & G.12 also special attention on G.12 & G.5. By group retaliated for artillery fire & checked suspected position of trench mortar.	
	2/5/16		Enemy artillery again active against our trenches in G.11, G.5, G.11 & G.12. HULLUCH ALLEY & STANSFIELD ROAD were also attacked. By 4.7mm from 2.30h to 3.0pm. Right Group retaliated again checked suspected position of Trench mortar. Between 10·45 & 11·30 p.m. C/42 fired in retribution for hostile trench howitzer & rifle grenades. Enemy been silenced by D/42 at 2·15pm, when firing at our aeroplane. Between 9.20 & 9.31am enemy field guns shelled ammunition pieces from G.12.c.5.8. to G.12.d.1.3. B/42 retaliated. The enemy artillery continued active during the day, and at 4·40pm they shot burst sun flame and occasionally for three minutes the bombardment continued, but was violently on till 11.40pm.	

SECRET

Army Form C. 2118.

WAR DIARY or INTELLIGENCE SUMMARY.

40th Bde R.F.A. (Right Group)

(Erase heading not required.)

Instructions regarding War Diaries and Intelligence Summaries are contained in F. S. Regs., Part II. and the Staff Manual respectively. Title pages will be prepared in manuscript.

Place	Date	Hour	Summary of Events and Information	Remarks and references to Appendices
Philosophe	3/5/16 4/5/16		A shallow trench is being dug from Sap at G.5.d.5.3 to G.5.d.2.24.6. At 4.50 am enemy shelled our support trenches about G.11 central with fuse gun. During 2-3 day there has been intermittent shelling of our trenches in G.11. Minenwerfers have also been occasionally active. Right group assisted several time registered during the day shooting fairly dispersed by B/42 in G.6.4. D/42 fired at unknown guns in the QUARRIES' which were firing at our aeroplanes. During raid at dusk observed. Respirator O.P. where movement has been observed, fired at in D/42 burning to kill. Light gun peals were not obtained from work appears to have been done an O.P. a slip of water near G.12 a G.5.	
	5/5/16		Between 8am & 9am the enemy shelled G.11 a. & G.11c. with H.E.'s about 200 shells. Further intermittent shelling of G.11 & G.12 during the day. By Batteries retaliated. B''/43 shelled	

SECRET

Army Form C. 2118.

Instructions regarding War Diaries and Intelligence Summaries are contained in F. S. Regs., Part II. and the Staff Manual respectively. Title pages will be prepared in manuscript.

WAR DIARY or INTELLIGENCE SUMMARY.

40th Bde R.F.A. (Right Group)

(Erase heading not required.)

Place	Date	Hour	Summary of Events and Information	Remarks and references to Appendices
Pulverches	3/5/16		Trench Mortar's on special position. "A"/42 registered several points by aerial observation. No hostile break has been successfully replied to. G 5 d 3.6. Enemy heard hard at work repairing damage done in yesterday's bombardment on B"c of "A"/40 fired & dispersed working parties. Between 8.10 & 8.45 am, enemy shelled P.12.c	R.R.
	4/5/16		CHAPEL ALLEY and DEVON LANE with 4.2's. 4pm – 10.15 am & 2pm to 1.40pm the enemy shelled P.11 with 5.9's intermittently. At 3.20pm the enemy shelled P.5.c & G.11.B.d heavily. Right Group artillery retaliated, for artillery on Trench B8 & P9 action shelling. Several points registered.	
			At 1-1.15 am enemy shelled P.11.B & P.5.b with about 30 5.9's. 4.2's active during the morning on B.11.a & G.11.d. At 9.20am Trench Mortars in vicinity of QUARRIES active on G.12.c. B/43 retaliated & the trench mortars ceased firing. During the day the enemy artillery has been	R.R.

1577   Wt. W10791/1773   500,000   1/15   D.D. & L.   A.D.S.S./Forms/C. 2118.

SECRET

Army Form C. 2118.

Instructions regarding War Diaries and Intelligence Summaries are contained in F. S. Regs., Part II. and the Staff Manual respectively. Title pages will be prepared in manuscript.

WAR DIARY or INTELLIGENCE SUMMARY.

70th Bde R.F.A. (Right Group)

(Erase heading not required.)

Place	Date	Hour	Summary of Events and Information	Remarks and references to Appendices
Philosophe	4/5/16		normally active. My battery retaliated.	
	5/5/16		During the day G.11 & G.12 have been shelled by the enemy's artillery. Between 2.10pm and 3.25pm hostile trench mortar shelled P.5.d.0.4. and P.5.d.1.2. The howitzer's position was located at or near P.5.d.3.4/3. each time it fired "A"/40 fired on the trench mortar position each occasion the mortar ceased firing only 4 rounds in all a little later B/43 observed a field position of hostile trench mortar at the QUARRIES about G.12.a.5.4. Enemy Artillery active today against G.11 & G.12. particularly P.11. between 9.15am & 10.20am they put about 80 5.9's into this square or P.5. by Right Group. 6 batteries retaliated fiercely throughout 18 enemy TM's between 1.15pm opening fire were dispersed at P.5.d.4.3.6 by A"/40. At 6pm D/42 dispersed & partly & men behind the trench this trenches B/43 again aggressive against mm. supers in G.12.a.	fig. fig. fig.

SECRET

Army Form C. 2118.

WAR DIARY or INTELLIGENCE SUMMARY

Right Group R.F.A. 70th Bde R.F.A.

(Erase heading not required.)

Instructions regarding War Diaries and Intelligence Summaries are contained in F.S. Regs., Part II. and the Staff Manual respectively. Title pages will be prepared in manuscript.

Place	Date	Hour	Summary of Events and Information	Remarks and references to Appendices
Philosophe	10/5/16		Rd. Hdn ent H.1½ am an enemy minenwerfer extimated about R.12a central opened fire on our trenches in G.11.b. "D"/43 or each minenwerfer ly fly pdr gun or G.11.a central. During the day the enemy lt fly pdr gun or M.2's have been active against our trenches in G.11 & G.12. "B" Battery retaliated. "B"/43 fired on working party in RITE ST. ELIE. party dispersed. "C"/43 fired on ranging working party at H.1 & 6.0. Retaliation was carried out by batteries.	R.1.
	11/5/16		B. 8.30am & 10.25am, the enemy shelled G.11.a & G.11.b with 5.9's B. & 10.20am & 1.10pm M.11.b was shelled with light field gun & 4.25 am & 2.45pm about 30 5.9 shells were fired into G.8.c.6.6 A/40 retaliated at 8.30am by shelling G.5 & G.11.1	
		4pm	The enemy opened a heavy bombardment on our front trenches from HOHENZOLLERN to the QUARRIES also in VERMELLES and PHILOSOPHE, with all descriptions of shells from my lt field guns to 8" Howitzers. All batteries opened fire on their	R.1

SECRET

Right Group WAR DIARY or R.F.A. (40th Bde R.F.A.)
INTELLIGENCE SUMMARY.
Army Form C. 2118.

Place	Date	Hour	Summary of Events and Information	Remarks and references to Appendices
Philosophe	11/5/16		Allotted Zones. "A"/42 & "B"/42 were restricted to search zones & approaches in H.1. "B"/43 wiped Communication trenches in H.1. about 6 p.m. the following ranges were not exceeded— "D"/42 from G.5.c.6.8. to G.5.c.6.8. "B"/42 from G.5.c.6.8. to G.5.c.0.6. "C"/42 from G.11.b.8.6. to H.7.c.1.1. "A"/42 was moved to Guildale on to G.5.d.5.5. to G.5.d.4/2.0. The Howitzers were given single re-cutting points in support line behind Battery Zones. Owing to the destruction of telephone wires failure of communication the barrage of "A"/42 was not carried out & the Howitzers continued firing on H.1. All five the bombardment diminished in intensity, gradually dropping off until it finally finished at 9 p.m. Group Hd. Qrs Office was destroyed by 8" Howitzer Shell about 6 p.m. and was subsequently moved to batteries were either overrun by enemy or subsequently met. "A"/40 between the hours of 4 p.m. & 9 p.m. fired H.E. 2 A & 1 H.E. A x on G.5.d.5.5. to G.5.d.4/2.0.	

SECRET

WAR DIARY
or
INTELLIGENCE SUMMARY

Army Form C. 2118

RIGHT GROUP R.F.A. (404 Bee R.F.A.)

Instructions regarding War Diaries and Intelligence Summaries are contained in F.S. Regs, Part II. and the Staff Manual respectively. Title Pages will be prepared in manuscript.

(Erase heading not required.)

Place	Date	Hour	Summary of Events and Information	Remarks and references to Appendices
Philosophe	11/5/16		About 9 p.m. all batteries were put on their night lines, and during the night, at irregular intervals, rally shoots were made (rifles, Road, X tracks in rear of their own lines). The total amount of ammunition fired by the Group to 2.1, X83A. 880 AX. a 355 BX.	
	12/5/16		At 6.10 a.m. Enemy shelled our trench in P.11.b. 2".110mm a Trench howitzer old Rhine. Between 1.45 pm to 3.30 pm our trenches in P.11.a. & b were heavily shelled with 5.9's, 4.2's & high field guns. Between 4.45 pm trench howitzer was again active on P.11.a. Between 8.45 pm – 9.15 pm about 100 5.9 shells were fired at our trenches in P.11.a & b. Batteries retaliating. Several points registered.	
	13/5/16		During the day H.E. Germans again shelled our trenches in P.11.b. & P.11. with high velocity guns, 4.2's & 5.9's. Batteries retaliated "A"/43 on "A"/42 fired on obtained working parties at 6.5 & 6.5 & P.9.b.1/2.9.h. respectively. "B"/43 again engaged hirenenper in Quarries & trench 59 on fuze from at B.11.a. & P.11.a. whereupon, fired by the Germans on the 11th inst.	
	14/5/16		Trench howitzers again active against P.11.d. "B"/43 retaliated each time, firing on enemy's occupied positions. VERMELLES has been shelled intermittently during the day.	

1875 Wt. W593/826 1,000,000 4/15 J.B.C. & A. A.D.S.S./Forms/C. 2118.

SECRET

Right Group WAR DIARY R.H.A. (70th & 1 Bde R.H.A.)
or
INTELLIGENCE SUMMARY
(Erase heading not required.)

Place	Date	Hour	Summary of Events and Information
Philosophe	11/5/16		Batteries retaliated. The following howitzer wire been arranged on:— 4pm 12.20pm to 7.57pm:—
			"A"/40 from G.5.c.9.6. to G.5.d.1.4. A/42 G.5.d.6½.2. to G.11.d.8.6.
			B/42 G.5.d.5.3½. to G.5.d.6½.2. C/42 G.5.d.3.5. to G.5.d.5.3½.
			D/42 G.5.d.1.4. to G.5.d.3.5. B/43:— G.5.c.9.6. to G.5.d.6½.3.
			G.11.d.8.6. to G.5.d.6.2½.
			From 2pm to 4pm "A"/40 shelled enemy trench with shrapnel
			+H.E. from 6.15pm to 8.30pm G.5.d.2.6 to G.5.d.11.11½. 10.10pm there
			at G.5.d.2.3. "A"/42 between 6.15pm + 8.15pm shelled
			G.11.d.9.6 to G.11.d.8.6. G.5.d.4.0. to G.11.d.9.6. "C"/42 G.5.d.5½.2½.
			to G.5.d.4.0. "D"/42 G.5.d.4.4½. to G.5.d.5½.2½. "B"/43 from 6.15pm
			to 4pm G.5.d.3½.4½. to G.5.d.5.5. G.5.d.4.4. G.5.d.8.2½. G.5.d.9½.11½.
			+ G.11.d.9½.8½. from 4pm to 8pm G.5.d.3½.6½. G.5.d.4.4. Enemy R.J.
			G.5.d.8.2½. G.5-d.9½.8½. at 1.30pm Enemy
			replied in turn near the Queries.
12/5/16			At 5.10pm a considerable amount of expressed in G.u.b. there
			was no reply on their fire. At 10pm tonight a wine was
			erected at G.u.d. Heavy rifle + machine gun fire followed
			Enemy Artillery fairly quiet during the day, at 10.10pm
			he shelled G.11.A. with 5·9c.m 2·5c. + 4·4cm Batteries
			retaliated. "A"/40 dispersed working party at G.5.d.3.5. at
			9.49pm also on sd. G.5.c.9.5 a short mn.

SECRET

Right Group WAR DIARY or R.F.A. INTELLIGENCE SUMMARY
(40th Bde R.F.A.)

Army Form C. 2118

Instructions regarding War Diaries and Intelligence Summaries are contained in F.S. Regs., Part II. and the Staff Manual respectively. Title Pages will be prepared in manuscript.

(Erase heading not required.)

Place	Date	Hour	Summary of Events and Information	Remarks and references to Appendices
Philosophe	16/3/16		Enemy artillery active against our trenches in G.11 c.12, particularly G.11 Right Group batteries retaliated effectively. Several points of new construction of new earthwork is believed that an under note for fresh activity is being observed.	
	19/3/16		Enemy artillery trench mortar emplacement on the hostile front line trenches in the district of the Tamines — a fire from the Rouerie to the kink. Batteries retaliated during the works sufficiently. Enemy observed much damage to hostile works occurred by our Howitzer Batteries. Registration guns. Registrations	
	19/3/16		Enemy artillery trench mortars active today, our latter trench replenished. Retaliation performed.	
	20/3/16		Hostile Artillery gun active also Trench Mortars by fire too times been begun to also by B/42 Batteries & further by B.B. judging that also helped active against new trenches in G.11 & G.12. Enemy Batteries registered active also by A/42. shrapnel of an inch to impound a working party in G.12	
	21/3/16		Enemy artillery appeared to be 5.9's, trench hostile tor, also helped active against our trenches in G.11 & G.12. Enemy Batteries registered behind enemy lines by A/42. which shrapnel also zipped to impound a working party in G.11 H.F.A.D.S.	
	22/3/16		G.11 & G.12 again shelled by guns mortars unknown during the day. Our Howitzer retaliation Enemy light fired	

SECRET

Ryl. Group or R.F.A. (70th 1 Bde RFA)

WAR DIARY or INTELLIGENCE SUMMARY

Army Form C. 2118

(Erase heading not required.)

Instructions regarding War Diaries and Intelligence Summaries are contained in F.S. Regs., Part II. and the Staff Manual respectively. Title Pages will be prepared in manuscript.

Place	Date	Hour	Summary of Events and Information	Remarks and references to Appendices
Ph.Josophe	22/5/16		Gun battery has been directed today by O/y.2 at H3.a.2.9 during the night, a few rounds were fired from the new line, otherwise new line battery E.S.I.T. being engaged continuously. Owing there was a signal to aeroplanes as during the evening and nights the observer to be dropped from 'plane over our lines.	
	23/5/16		Trench no G.11 and G.12 again engaged the artillery of Owens Antiwerp. (Ryh Quen glas + S.9's) Our Artillery was obliged to retaliate freely. B/y.3 engaged completed firesweeps & anti-aircraft battery during the day & when guns firing at new aeroplane. Very quiet in the afternoon during the day.	
	24/5/16		Enemy Artillery again active, also trench howitzer on our trenches in G.11 & G.12. B/y.3 fired at enemy position at Trunkuline each time they fired, was such observation they seemed free. Several working parties behind enemy lines dispersed during the day. There were reports the evening at 6.58pm + 8.50pm opposite St Eloi of the Cheveaux-de-frise inflated then was duck looking moving. A rifle fire to movement need to be observed.	

1875. Wt. W593/826 1,000,000 4/15 J.B.C. & A. A.D.S.S./Forms/C. 2118.

SECRET

Right Group R.F.A.
(40th Bde R.F.A.) Army Form C. 2118

WAR DIARY
or
INTELLIGENCE SUMMARY
(Erase heading not required.)

Instructions regarding War Diaries and Intelligence Summaries are contained in F. S. Regs., Part II. and the Staff Manual respectively. Title Pages will be prepared in manuscript.

Place	Date	Hour	Summary of Events and Information	Remarks and references to Appendices
Philosophe	25/5/16		Enemy Trench mortars active this morning between 3.35 & 5.30 p.m., opened an burst in G.11.b. B/43 retaliated as requested. Fraction of Trench mortars. The wiring at Enemy M.G. emplacement in F.R. opposite we have approved South of Pits 13 observed. Checked also G.11.b. During	
	26/5/16		early afternoon by B/42 this after Enemy Trench mortar Observing Stations were extremely active during the day. We also communicated to them as they were opened. Enemy Trench mortars were 10 days. Possibly type of this have reposed at 4.5" pm. a/b at 9 h. 32 then Nr a were responded at 4.5" pm.	
	27/5/16		In firing by B/43 four days reported disturbances of the enemy trenches. Trench mortars and rifle grenades has been engaged vigorously in several occasions during the day.	
	28/5/16		At 3 a.m. this morning we observed the Enemy hard supported. We also set communication trenches in Hanna railway in the opening a heavy fire and three guns to trench sections. The latter however were silenced immediately followed by our M.S.S. These guns have been dispersed through the day.	
	29/5/16		Enemy Artillery Trench mortars have been rather more active than war before has done a good deal of	

SECRET

WAR DIARY or INTELLIGENCE SUMMARY

Army Form C. 2118

Right & Left (70th Bde R.F.A.) R.F.A.

Vol 9

Instructions regarding War Diaries and Intelligence Summaries are contained in F. S. Regs., Part II. and the Staff Manual respectively. Title Pages will be prepared in manuscript.

(Erase heading not required.)

Place	Date	Hour	Summary of Events and Information	Remarks and references to Appendices
Philosophe	29/5/16		retaliation. at 2.30 am an enemy ammunition dump in rear trenches was blown up by our trench mortars who fired at our trenches. This caused some damage to S.P. 8.	
	30/5/16		Heavy Artillery again active against enemy trenches in G.11 c. & G.12.	R.
	31/5/16		A when our opponents experiments engages by our batteries. Several very successful shoots. Enemy Artillery never active having its covering trench mortars with trench mortars, ordered to bombard roaged up to be seen 200 lbs in weight on enemy G.R. Selbiaztine.	

MA Christie
Lt Col

WAR DIARY

C/70th BRIGADE R. F. A.

May

1916.

Army Form C. 2118.

WAR DIARY
or
INTELLIGENCE SUMMARY. *Bryotha Ftd* May Vol 1
(Erase heading not required.)

Instructions regarding War Diaries and Intelligence Summaries are contained in F. S. Regs., Part II. and the Staff Manual respectively. Title pages will be prepared in manuscript.

Place	Date	Hour	Summary of Events and Information	Remarks and references to Appendices
MANNEQUIN	1/5/16	6.20	Fired on PERSIVAL ALLEY & FOSSE ALLEY in reply to German trench Mortars on G.S.C.	
		1.07pm	Fired on G.S.A.3.M for enemy shelling our trenches in G.S.C. N° of rounds fired during day 12A 20AX8	
	2/5/16	12.45/2pm 1.15	Enemy shelling our trenches in G.S.C. Retaliated on POTSDAM TRENCH and FOSSE ALLEY.	
		9.20 pm	Joined in Battalion + Trench Mortar shoot by firing on ZEPPLIN and PERSIVAL ALLEY, enemy retaliated on our front line in G.S.C, we counter retaliated on POTSDAM TRENCH N° of rounds fired during day 22A 13AX	
	3/5/16	7.40 am	Enemy fired on our front and outpost line in G.S.C. Retaliated on POTSDAM TRENCH and junction of FOSSE ALLEY	
		9.5 am	Slight shelling of our front line in G.S.C. & D. retaliated on POTSDAM TRENCH	

Army Form C. 2118.

WAR DIARY
or
INTELLIGENCE SUMMARY.
(Erase heading not required.)

B/70 Bde RFA (2)

Instructions regarding War Diaries and Intelligence Summaries are contained in F. S. Regs., Part II. and the Staff Manual respectively. Title pages will be prepared in manuscript.

Place	Date	Hour	Summary of Events and Information	Remarks and references to Appendices
	3/8/16	11.0 am	Trench mortars on BORDER REDOUBT, retaliated on G.5.d.4.6. to G.5.d.4.4. to G.5.d.3.7.	
		2.40 pm	Enemy fired 7 trench mortars on our trenches in G.5.C retaliated on POTSDAM TRENCH.	
		3.20	Large trench mortar on our trenches in G.5.C retaliated on POTSDAM TRENCH.	
		4.25 pm	Enemy fired large trench mortar on our trenches in G.5.C retaliated on POTSDAM TRENCH.	
		4.40	Enemy shelled our front support trenches very heavily in G.5.C + D. for 15 minutes. Retaliated on POTSDAM TRENCH	
		5.40	Enemy shelling our trenches in G.5.C with large trench mortars, retaliated on POTSDAM TRENCH and junction of FOSSE ALLEY + CHINA TRENCH.	
		6.40	Fired on trenches G.6.c.2.9. to G.6.a.8.2. as Germans were reported moving there, our trenches in G.5.C were at the same time shelled for about 10 minutes. NB 14 rounds fired during day 22 A 34 AX?	

Army Form C. 2118.

WAR DIARY
or
INTELLIGENCE SUMMARY.
(Erase heading not required.)

B/70 Bde R.F.A. (3)

Instructions regarding War Diaries and Intelligence Summaries are contained in F. S. Regs., Part II. and the Staff Manual respectively. Title pages will be prepared in manuscript.

Place	Date	Hour	Summary of Events and Information	Remarks and references to Appendices
	4-5-16	9-59 a.m.	Enemy fired on our trenches for 10 mins in G.11.A. retaliated on G.6.C.	
		4-30 pm	Bombarded POTSDAM trench ZEPPELIN ALLEY 73 A 14 A X? No 4 rounds fired during day	
	5-5-16	5.00 am	Enemy fired Rifle Grenades & Trench Mortars on our trenches in G.5.C for 40 Minutes. Retaliated on POTSDAM trench & POSSE ALLEY	
		6.0 a.m	Enemy exploded a large Mine in G.5.C.	
		8.0 am	Enemy fired into our front line in G.5.C	
		8.30 am	Enemy Artillery Activity on our front line	
		9.0 am to 9.15 am	retaliated about	
		7-15 pm	Enemy fired Shrapnel on STANSFIELD ROAD retaliated on G.6.D.14	
		7.25 pm	A few shrapnel on our trench in G.5.C. retaliated on POTSDAM trench & ZEPPELIN ALLEY	
			No it round fired during day 117 A 59 A X?	
	6-5-16	0 am	After persistent Shrapnel at STANSFIELD ROAD	
		10-10 am	Enemy shelled our trenches intermittently	
		to 11-50 am		

WAR DIARY or INTELLIGENCE SUMMARY.

(Erase heading not required.)

Army Form C. 2118.

B/70 Bde R.F.A. (4)

Place	Date	Hour	Summary of Events and Information	Remarks and references to Appendices
	6-5-16	10 pm 10.30 pm	Bombarded Front Line trench in G.5.D & C. Also trenches then caused retaliation which did not cause relation.	
	7-5-16	7-10 am 7-30 am	No. of rounds fired during day 73 A. 40 A.X? Enemy shelled our trenches in vicinity of G.11.A. retaliated on Enemy front line in G.5.D.	
		8.05 pm to 9.15 pm	Enemy shelled our trenches in G.5.D 6.3 G.5.D 7.3.2	
		9.05 am to 9.30 am	Enemy shelled our trenches in G.11.B. retaliated on G.5.D 6.3 - Y G.5.D 7.3.2	
		9.30 am 10.30 am	Enemy shelled our Infantry in G.5.C. retaliated on G.5.D 4.7 G.5.D 2.6 Y.9.5	
		10.45 am	Enemy shelled Archer trench retaliated on G.5.D 2.6 Y.9.5 D 2.3.6.5	
		11-7.50 am 11-11.25 am 11.25 am to 12 noon	Enemy shelled our trenches in G.5.C with 7th 4.2 H.S in G.5.C retaliated on G.5.C.9.7.8.5 & G.5.D.7.1 G.5.D 3.5	
		12.30 pm	Retaliated for Trench Mortar 4th 2nd in G.5.C	

WAR DIARY or INTELLIGENCE SUMMARY. B/70 Bde R.F.A. (5)

Army Form C. 2118.

Place	Date	Hour	Summary of Events and Information	Remarks and references to Appendices
	9-5-16	12.45 pm to 1.30 pm	Occasional shell in G.5.C. retaliated on FOSSE ALLEY, CHINA TRENCH & junction in G.6.C.	
			N° of Rounds fired during day 39 A-62 AX.	
	9-5-16	4.00 am to 4.30 am	Light Trench Mortar on our front & support in G.5.C.Y.D retaliated on POTSDAM TRENCH	
		6.10 am	Enemy shelling on POTSDAM TRENCH	
		6.45 am to	Enemy shelling our front line in G.5.D. retaliated in TRENCH. Bombardment continued till 9.10 am retaliated in enemy front line	
		9.30 am 10.9.45 am	5 – 9" & 17 MM on G.11.B. retaliated on G.5.D.7.4 & G.5.D.6.3.	
		11.15 am	Rifle Grenades on our front line in G.5.D. swept enemy front line on G.5.D.2.6. to G.5.D.6.3.	
		11.40 am	5-9" on CROWN TRENCH I KINK retaliated on G.5.D.2.6.	
		10.12.0 Noon 1.25 pm	Shrapnel gr G.5.C. retaliated on PERSIVAL & ZEPP ALLEY	
		3.40 pm	Rifle Grenades on STANSFIELD ROAD retaliated on G.5.D.7.4	
			No rounds fired during day. 50 A 90 AX	
	9-5-16	8.30 am 10.10 am	Enemy heavy shelling on our ZONE by 5-9" retaliated on Enemy front line	

WAR DIARY
or
INTELLIGENCE SUMMARY. B/170 Bde RFA (6)

Army Form C. 2118.

Place	Date	Hour	Summary of Events and Information	Remarks and references to Appendices
	9.8.16		During afternoon Enemy fired light French Mortar on our front, retaliated on Enemy's front line. No of rounds fired during day. 5 H.A. 65 A.X.	
		10.45 -61.45 pm	Zone very quiet. About 1.45 pm a few H.E. & Trench Mortars fired on our front line	
		6.20 pm	Enemy opened on our front line in B.5.C & D. retaliated on Enemy front line	
		7.10 pm	Enemy fired on our front line in B.5.C.9D. Retaliated on Enemy front line. No of rounds fired during day. 70 A 73 AX	
			5 Hy French Mortars on Rifleman's Alley. Retaliated on G.5.D.55.	
	11.5.16	4.40 am	Artly Heavy bombardment German troops in our front line line in B.& D.1 & C.& D.12. I also Anchor Trench & Crown Trench opened on Hulloch	
		3-6 pm	Alley, kept up a barrage until 4.0 am 12-5-16 to support counter attack	
			No of rounds fired during day 1000 A 800 AX	

WAR DIARY
or
INTELLIGENCE SUMMARY B/70 Bde R.F.A. (1)

Army Form C. 2118.

Instructions regarding War Diaries and Intelligence Summaries are contained in F. S. Regs., Part II. and the Staff Manual respectively. Title pages will be prepared in manuscript.

Place	Date	Hour	Summary of Events and Information	Remarks and references to Appendices
	12-5-16		Shot Staff M.T.L. 5.9" & 7.7 M.M. on our new line retaliated accordingly. No of rounds fired during day 318 A 237 AX?	
	13-5-16		Slight shelling mostly registration retaliated heavily 20A 161 AX. No of rounds fired during day	
	14-5-16	12-20 pm	Germans during news from line the front of Anchor Trench during night. Bombarded Enemys new front line, & B07 au 99	
		10.15 am	for intending attack which was stopped by Bosch	
		6.0 pm		
		7.0 & 3 pm		
		9.50.10		
		10.30 pm	Fired on B07 au 99 then B07 au 100 till 11-0 am	
			No of rounds fired during day 325A 300 AX	
	15-5-16 8-50 am		Were heavily near G.4. D.77 Cristoru practically the same on left, harrassed fires a little.	
			No of rounds fires during day 70 A 75 AX.	
	16-5-16		Line changed to G.12 A.4 3 3/4 G.5 D.9 8.2 most the Battalion of a few registration fires were quiet.	

WAR DIARY
or
INTELLIGENCE SUMMARY. B/70 Bde R.F.A.

Army Form C. 2118.

Place	Date	Hour	Summary of Events and Information	Remarks and references to Appendices
	16-5-16	6.0 pm	Supporting right Battalion of Left Brigade. No. of rounds fired during day 10A ?	
	17-5-16		Occasion shelling during day.	
		6.30 pm	Are bombarded for ½ hour in retaliation for enemy heavy bombardment. No. of rounds fires during day 138A 112AX ?	
	18-5-16		Heavy shelling after shortfall on our trenches on G.11.B. Retaliated on QUARRY TRENCH during afternoon remarkably quiet. No. of rounds fired during day. 66 A, 39 A.X.	
	19-5-16		Occasional Rifle grenades on our front line, retaliates on enemy front line.	
		9.30 am 10.9.40 am	Greenewell 4" & 2" M. M. trench mortars in G.11.A retaliates on enemys trenches in G.5.D. No. of rounds fired during day 14 A 16 A.X.	
	20-5-16		Registered new communicating line. No. of rounds fired during day. 10A 5AX	

Army Form C. 2118.

WAR DIARY
or
INTELLIGENCE SUMMARY
(Erase heading not required.)

13/70 Bde R.F.A. (9)

Place	Date	Hour	Summary of Events and Information	Remarks and references to Appendices
	21-5-16	9.45am 11-40am 2.20pm	Enemy fired 150th field guns on our front line G.11.B. retaliated on Enemy front line & supports. Nest rounds fired during day. 16A 3AX? Fairly quiet, nothing except for an occasional 2cm. tt. trench Mortar on our trenches near B0740 9+. 1st field gun regulating our front line in G.11.B. retaliated heavily in Enemy front line	
	22-5-16		No of rounds fired during day 2/A 3/AX? Heavy trench Mortar bombardment mostly on N.L. Regd. & left of No. 2. also Rifle grenades on Border Redoubt & Sackville St. retaliated heavily & damaged Enemy parapet. No of rounds fires during day 49A 29AX?	
	23-5-16		Rifle grenades registered on new trenches along Rifle Grenade N. Border Redoubt. retaliated on trenches G.12.A. Heavy trench Mortar on Clifford St. & B0740 10 4. retaliated 44A 25AX? No of rounds fired during day	
	24-5-16			

WAR DIARY or INTELLIGENCE SUMMARY

Army Form C. 2118.

13/70 Bde R.F.A. (10)

Place	Date	Hour	Summary of Events and Information	Remarks and references to Appendices
	25-5-16		Field Gun registered our trenches Rifle Grenades on B.07.a.0.97 retaliated over whole Zone. Enemy Shelled our Front Line with Field Gun retaliated on enemy Front Line. No. of rounds fired during day 30.A. 20.A.X.?	
	26-5-16		Trench Mortar duels during day, also field guns fired on our trenches in G.11.b, retaliated on enemy trenches. No. of rounds fired during day 45.A. 6.A.X.	
	27-5-16		Enemy Shelled gun trenches for one hour with 2" T. Mortar. Rep. request on our support line in G.11.B. 2 heavy trench Mortars near B.07.a.94, retaliated on enemy trenches. No. of rounds fired during day 85.A. 60.A.X.	
	28-5-16		Enemy Shelled V.60.S. & Kaiserin trench, Rifle Grenades fired on SACKVILLE St. Field gun registering new trenches G.11.A, retaliated sweeping trenches in G.12.A. & G.11.B. No. of rounds fired during day 50.A. 20.A.X.	

WAR DIARY or INTELLIGENCE SUMMARY. B/70 Bde R.F.A. (11)

Army Form C. 2118.

Place	Date	Hour	Summary of Events and Information	Remarks and references to Appendices
	29.5.16	3.45am	Enemy swept our trenches in G.11.B.1, G.11.A for 5 minutes. Retaliated in G.12.A.2.4 registered guns replied. CZ ZERO line on G5D4th night line.	
		10.40am	Heavy Trench Mortars on our trenches in G.11.B. Retaliated on Enemy front line + Quarries.	
		10.45am	Enemy bombarded our front trenches in G.11.B, G.11.A G.11.B. rapidly. Retaliated on Enemy trenches in G.11.B. G.12.A. during afternoon. Enemy bombarded front + communication trenches with 8 Round for four. Enemy were refused to fire.	
	30.5.16	2.58am	Not round-fired through. Enemy Communication trenches shelled. G.12.B½.7½, G.12.A.2.7, G.12.B.½.5½, G.12.A.7.3	104.A. 119.AX. G.6.C.4.1, G.6.C.O.1.
		3.4am	Enemy shelled our front line in G5 D1 C1A. Retaliated	G5 D1 C1A. Retaliated
		3.30am	on Enemys trenches	
		7.30am	A few 4.2" on our trenches in G.12.A. swept G5 D.7.0.	

WAR DIARY or INTELLIGENCE SUMMARY.

Army Form C. 2118.

B/70 B.H.R.F.A (2)

(Erase heading not required.)

Instructions regarding War Diaries and Intelligence Summaries are contained in F. S. Regs., Part II. and the Staff Manual respectively. Title pages will be prepared in manuscript.

Place	Date	Hour	Summary of Events and Information	Remarks and references to Appendices
		5.46 am	Fired on working party in HAIRPIN CRATERS, field gun registered G40D	
		10 to 4.30pm	Intermittent shelling of our zone with field gun. No reply. Fresh during day 43.A 46 AX	
		9.5 to 9.20am	A few H.E. squeak on our trench	
		1.15 am	5 "9" fired on LANCER LANE & CROWN TRENCH, retaliated on G.6.C + G.12.A	
		11.15 am	Field Gun fired on BORDER REDOUBT retaliated on saps or selected trench in G.5.D.	
		4.15 pm	Fired in support of aeroplane during afternoon. No rifle fired during day C33.A. 44 AX	

Army Form C. 2118.

WAR DIARY
or
INTELLIGENCE SUMMARY.
(Erase heading not required.)

Instructions regarding War Diaries and Intelligence Summaries are contained in F. S. Regs., Part II. and the Staff Manual respectively. Title pages will be prepared in manuscript.

C/70

Place	Date	Hour	Summary of Events and Information	Remarks and references to Appendices
	1916			
Vermelles	1st May		Fired 18 A. 26 Ax. Fired on front line in G5c at request of infantry at 9.40 p.m. company concerned reported favourably as to the effects of our fire.	MMS
	2nd May		Fired 62 A : registered points G5a 2.5 and G5a 1,2½ by aeroplane	MMS
	3rd May		" 50 A & 48 Ax : Registered trench junction at G5c 39 and G5c 6½ 8½ by aeroplane.	MMS
	4th May		" 20 A 67 Ax : registered Machine gun emplacements G5c 6½ 6½, French G5c 4½ 8, Trench A 29 d 8.5 'stand to' at 4 am. Cancelled. Capt H Armytage proceeded on leave	MMS
	5th May		" 63 A 88 Ax	MMS
	6th May		185 A 93 Ax Retaliated at request of infantry	MMS
	7th May		41 A 14 Ax	MMS
	8th May		Quiet day	MMS

Army Form C. 2118.

WAR DIARY
or
INTELLIGENCE SUMMARY.
(Erase heading not required.)

Instructions regarding War Diaries and Intelligence Summaries are contained in F. S. Regs., Part II. and the Staff Manual respectively. Title pages will be prepared in manuscript.

Place	Date	Hour	Summary of Events and Information	Remarks and references to Appendices
Vermelles	1916 9th May		Fired 98 A 50 Ax	MM8
	10th "		" 65 A 75 Ax	MM8
	11th "		Fired before noon 147 A 166 Ax ; between noon & next morning fired 1294 A and 403 Ax. About 3:30 p.m. enemy opened heavy barrage on front of support trenches, also onto Vermelles. Continued till about 5 p.m. when it 'lifted' onto communication & reserve trenches. An infantry attack was then launched, which left the enemy in possession of our front & support trenches by Hussar Horn; our new front line becoming Vigo St – Sackville St – Hulluch Alley – Began 99. An barrage kept up at varying rate till early next morning (12th). No 94749 Gunner C Mitchell, No 1 No 1 gun killed about 8 a.m. while in Gun pit by splinter of high velocity shell, which burst behind the pit.	MM8
	12th		Infantry H.Q. charged, then spent day firing green wrecked by shell & all occupants (N. Sec.No) killed or wounded on infantry occupied Anchor Trench but they were unable to hold it.	MM8
	13th		Fired 282 A 40 Ax : counter attack (on infantry)	MM8
			" 12 A 69 Ax	
	14th		" 265 A 255 Ax Divisional concentration of artillery on trenches taken by enemy started at 6 p.m. almost immediate heavy retaliation; our fire 'lifted' at 6.45 p.m. when two companies left our trenches. They reached Began 99 but were unable to hold it. Firing died down about 8:30 p.m.	MM8
	15th		Very quiet day; no firing	MM8

Army Form C. 2118.

WAR DIARY
or
INTELLIGENCE SUMMARY.
(Erase heading not required.)

Instructions regarding War Diaries and Intelligence
Summaries are contained in F. S. Regs., Part II.
and the Staff Manual respectively. Title pages
will be prepared in manuscript.

Place	Date May 1916	Hour	Summary of Events and Information	Remarks and references to Appendices
Vermelles	16th	Fixed 13 A 20 Ax	No 3 gun's dugout completed	MMS
	17th	" 80 A 80 Ax		MMS
	18th	" 4 A 22 Ax	Changed zone further south : new OP in Hulluch Alley	MMS
	19th	" 41 Ax		MMS
	20th	" 4 A		MMS
	21st	" 22 A 80 Ax	No 2 & 4 gun's dugouts now complete	MMS
	22nd	" 15 A 30 Ax		MMS
	23rd	" 17 A 90 Ax	2nd Lt McFoy posted away to A/70 ; 2nd Lt Donald posted from A/70	MMS
	24th	" 24 A 59 Ax		MMS
	25th	" 8 A 118 Ax		MMS
	26th	" 23 A 32 Ax	New Telephone dug out completed	MMS
	27th	" 20 A 27 Ax		MMS
	28th	" 75 A 35 Ax	To H/y 125th D.A. received 15th D.A. on account of information of deserter of coming gas attack : C/64 to come to us tomorrow	MMS
	29th	" 135 A 131 Ax	Organised bombardment of enemy front line, attempt to explode gas cylinders : unsuccessful	MMS
	30th	" 4 A 46 Ax		MMS
	31st	" — A 51 Ax		MMS
	1st June	29 A 89 A		MMS

H. Bunyku
Capt
Comdg 6/70 Bde RFA

Army Form C. 2118.

B/70 Bde R.F.A.

June Vol 2

WAR DIARY or INTELLIGENCE SUMMARY.

(Erase heading not required.)

Instructions regarding War Diaries and Intelligence Summaries are contained in F. S. Regs., Part II. and the Staff Manual respectively. Title pages will be prepared in manuscript.

Place	Date	Hour	Summary of Events and Information	Remarks and references to Appendices
	1/6/16	7.45 am	Retaliated on hos German trench in G.5.d. with C/70 in retaliation for light field gun shelling of our trenches G.11.b.	
		2.30 pm	KAISERIN TRENCH shelled with 77 M.M. also 5.9" on O.G.I & a few 4.2" on junction of HULLUCH ALLEY & HIGHLAND TRENCH, also heavy trench mortars about BOYAU 95	
		3.30 pm	About 3 minute concentrated firing on LANCER LANE with 77 M.M. a few Rifle Grenades in BORDER REDOUBT. No. of rounds fired during day 40 "A" 20 "X".	
	2/6/16	5.45 am	2. 5.9" between STEELE AVENUE & GOBEN ALLEY, later some shelling of VIGO STREET & heavy trench mortar on CLIFFORD STREET.	
		7.15 am	Retaliated for Rifle Grenade on BORDER REDOUBT	
		7.45 am	2. 4" on LANCER LANE. Retaliated on FOSSE ALLEY G.6.C.2.9 + G.5.6.8½.2.	
		8.0 am	Fired occasionally into machine gun emplacements in	

Army Form C. 2118.

B/70 Bde R.F.A. (2)

WAR DIARY
or
INTELLIGENCE SUMMARY.
(Erase heading not required.)

Instructions regarding War Diaries and Intelligence Summaries are contained in F. S. Regs., Part II. and the Staff Manual respectively. Title pages will be prepared in manuscript.

Place	Date	Hour	Summary of Events and Information	Remarks and references to Appendices
	2/6/16		G.6.A.II. & communication trenches in retaliation for Rifle Grenades on BORDER REDOUBT; also in support of aeroplanes.	
		6.30 pm 7.0 pm	A few Rifle Grenades on our front line & CROWN TRENCH about BOYAU 97. We retaliated	
	3/6/16	7.30 am	N° of rounds fired during day 12 "A" 56 "AX"	
			General fired a few shells on HIGHLAND TRENCH	
		1.0 pm	Enemy fired with minenwerfer onto SACKVILLE STREET and HULLUCH ALLEY, retaliated on ALEXANDER TRENCH from BOYAU 99 – BOYAU 100.	
		7.35 pm	A few H" Shrapnel on O.G.2. retaliated on G.12.a.1.6.2.	
			N° of rounds fired during day 19 "A"	
	4/6/16		Enemy fired with Light trenchmortars SACKVILLE STREET and HULLUCH ALLEY, retaliated on ALEXANDER TRENCH, between BOYAU 99 and 100.	
		4.5 pm	Three minenwerfer from QUARRIES on BOYAU 95, our trench mortars retaliated heavily	

WAR DIARY or INTELLIGENCE SUMMARY

Army Form C. 2118.

(Erase heading not required.)

Instructions regarding War Diaries and Intelligence Summaries are contained in F. S. Regs., Part II. and the Staff Manual respectively. Title pages will be prepared in manuscript.

Place	Date	Hour	Summary of Events and Information	Remarks and references to Appendices
	4/6/16	5.35 PM	Field guns from East of ST ELIE fired on STANSFIELD ROAD about G.10.a.3.0, retaliated on machine gun emplacement G.11.b.8½.9½.	
		6.0 pm	Fired on movement in G.6.c.2.9½.	
		8.5 pm	Fired on movement in G.6.c.2.9½. No. of rounds fired during day. 13 "A" 18 "AX"	
	5/6/16	7.30 am	We exploded a mine in G.H.4 and supported with shrapnel & Trench mortar, enemy retaliated on NORTHAMPTON TRENCH at 7.50 am 2 "d" on GOBEN ALLEY	
		7.45 am		
		9.35 am	Field guns from East of ST ELIE fired at STANSFIELD ROAD at observing stations about G.10.A.3.0. Retaliated on machine gun emplacement G.11.b.8½.9½.	
		9.50		
		11.35 am	A few trench mortars fell on our trenches in G.11.b, retaliated on suspected T.M. in G.12.a.7.2.	
		1.20 pm	Enemy fired a few 5.9" from direction of WINGLES on HULLUCH ALLEY & STANSFIELD ROAD in G.11.a. Retaliated on M.G. empt G.11.b.8½.9½. No. of rounds fired during day. 9 "A" 20 "AX"	

(4)

B/70 Bat R.F.A

Army Form C. 2118.

WAR DIARY
or
INTELLIGENCE SUMMARY.

(Erase heading not required.)

Instructions regarding War Diaries and Intelligence Summaries are contained in F.S. Regs., Part II. and the Staff Manual respectively. Title pages will be prepared in manuscript.

Place	Date	Hour	Summary of Events and Information	Remarks and references to Appendices
	6/6/16	7.0 am	A few H.E. 2" near GOBEN ALLEY.	
		7.30 am	A.4" shrapnel on O.G.1., our trench mortars have been firing bursts on B0YAU 96 + HAIRPIN CRATERS.	
		9.18 am	A few shrapnel on our front line G.11.b, Retaliated on	
		9.30 am	G.12.a.23.23. + G.6.a.3.0.	
		6.30 pm	Fired in support of bombing attack after explosion of British Mine at G.11.b.8.4½.	
			No. of rounds fired during day. 12. A 6 HX	
	7/6/16	5.0 am	Fired at registration of Infantry on Germans front line G.11.b.8.8½	
		6.0 am	Fired onto trench junction G.6.a.3.0. in retaliation for shelling of our reserve trench.	
		2.26 pm	Field guns fired occasionally on HULLUCH ALLEY	
		4.30 pm	Fired in support of aeroplane on FOSSE ALLEY about G.6.a. top 30.	
			Registering with aeroplane.	
			No. of rounds fired during day H6 "A" 3 "AX"	

1577 /Wt. W10791/1773 500,000 1/15 D. D. & L.   A.D.S.S./Forms/C. 2118.

(5)

B/70 Bde R.F.A.

Army Form C. 2118.

WAR DIARY
or
INTELLIGENCE SUMMARY.
(Erase heading not required.)

Place	Date	Hour	Summary of Events and Information	Remarks and references to Appendices
	8/6/16	7.40 am	Enemy shelled our trenches in G.11.b. intermittently. Retaliated on G.11.b. 8¾. 9¾.	
		7.55 am		
		9.50 am	Enemy a/gun shelled our front line from BORDER.	
			REDOUBT Southwards with field guns from BENIFONTAINE	
		12.30	Retaliated on G.11.b. 8¾. 9¾.	
		2.20 pm	Trench Mortar activity about B.0.Y+U 98 & 99.	
		3.28 pm	Two Trenty big Trench Mortars on BORDER REDOUBT, retaliated	
			on Trench about G.11.b. 8.9.	
		5.20 pm	Rifle Grenades on BORDER REDOUBT.	
		6.8 pm	Heavy Trench Mortars on BORDER REDOUBT, supported by 5"9"	
		6.35	on O.B.I. Junction with HULLUCH ALLEY & SACKVILLE STREET	
			Retaliated freely on G.11.c.9.8. Chin on hlight lines & supports	
			trench	
		8.0 pm	2 Minnie sprung at HAIRPIN by us, When retaliation came	
			we supported with shrapnel. THE over the craters all zones	
		8.20 pm		
			N° of rounds fired during day 16 A. SHAX	

(6)

Army Form C. 2118.

WAR DIARY
or
INTELLIGENCE SUMMARY.

(Erase heading not required.)

Instructions regarding War Diaries and Intelligence Summaries are contained in F. S. Regs., Part II. and the Staff Manual respectively. Title pages will be prepared in manuscript.

Place	Date	Hour	Summary of Events and Information	Remarks and references to Appendices
	9/6/16	7.50 am	Enemy fired on support line with field guns from WINGLES retaliated on front line G.11.b.8.6.	
		5.28 pm	A few shrapnel were fired on STANSFIELD ROAD & O.B.I junction	
		6.15 pm	2 heavy trench mortars in G.11.0.74. retaliated saw craters on trenches in G.11.6, the front line about G.11.6.89 has been blown in by G.2.2"	
		8.0 pm 8.15"	Fires at request of infantry in support of bombing attack on the German front line G.11.6.85 & G.12.A.14 after explosion of 2 large mines. No. of rounds fired during day 20 "A" 40 "H"	
	10/6/16	3.30 am	Mine went up in G.11.6.	
		2.15 pm	Mine went up to the right of PUITS 13.	
		3.0 pm	Our howrs on German support trenches in G.11.6 and also	
		3.30 pm	behind quarries enemy retaliated ring lights	
		3.55 pm	Registered German line in front of G.11.6.88.	
		4.10 pm	No. of rounds fired during day G "A" 16 "H"	

WAR DIARY or INTELLIGENCE SUMMARY.

Army Form C. 2118.

B/70Bde R.F.A.

(Erase heading not required.)

Instructions regarding War Diaries and Intelligence Summaries are contained in F.S. Regs., Part II. and the Staff Manual respectively. Title pages will be prepared in manuscript.

Place	Date	Hour	Summary of Events and Information	Remarks and references to Appendices
	11/6/16		Reinforcing detail relieved last night by section of C/175. Very quiet all day. No. of rounds fired during day "Nil"	
	12/6/16	5.30 am	Enemy shelled our trenches intermittently in G.11.b with trench mortars +H.2" Retaliated on lng:wire line	
		5.50 am		
		12.40 pm	Retaliated on trench junction G.11.b.9.7¾ for Leipsig trench Mortars, also retaliated on this point at 3.30 pm for Leipsig field gun firing on our trenches.	
		7.30 pm	5.9" fell on our trenches in G.11.b + G.11.a, retaliated on trench junction G.11.b.9.7¾. Light time from G.12.a.3.4 – G.5.a.7¾ t.	
		8.0 pm	No. of rounds fired during day. 5H."A" 20 H"A"	
	13/6/16	6.15 am	Enemy shelled our trenches in G.11.A + G.11.a with high field guns from W.IN.G.P.E.S, retaliated on trench junction G.5 @ 7¾.	
		9.30 am		
		2.30 pm	Enemy shelled our trenches in G.11. a + b with higher field guns	
		3.45 pm	No of rounds fired during day 15 "A"	

WAR DIARY or INTELLIGENCE SUMMARY

Army Form C. 2118.

B/70 Bde R.F.A.

Place	Date	Hour	Summary of Events and Information	Remarks and references to Appendices
	14/6/16	9.40 am	Enemy shelled GOBEN ALLEY with light howitzer guns from WINGLES retaliated on communication trench at G.11.b.83.5½.	
		9.50 am	Fired two salvos on ANCHOR TRENCH N° End of Group.	
		5.40 pm	Enemy fired on our trenches in G.11.A. retaliation G.11.b.83.5½.	
		7.40 pm	Enemy fired on our trenches in G.11.A. retaliated on G.11.b.83.5½.	
			N° of rounds fired during day 24 "A"	
	15/6/16	10.30 am	Slight shelling of our trenches in G.11.A. No reply given during rest of day.	
			N° of rounds fired during day 6 "A"	
	16/6/16	7.0 am	Enemy opened a very heavy machine gun & rifle fire on our aeroplanes. Right and C Group retaliated.	
		7-7 pm	Enemy fired heavily for 2 minutes on the trenches. Reply of gun fire Group 1 at G.11.b to G.12.C. retaliation communication trench & G.1.P.b.83.8.	
			Section of C/178 Bde retired C/185 Bde.	
			N° of rounds fired during day 4 "A"	

(9)

Army Form C. 2118.

WAR DIARY
or
INTELLIGENCE SUMMARY.
(Erase heading not required.)

Place	Date	Hour	Summary of Events and Information	Remarks and references to Appendices
	17/6/16	10.30 a.m.	Enemy aeroplane return our battery fired a few rounds from light field guns on SACKVILLE STREET.	
		3.0 p.m.	18 blew up two mines at S10 HAIRPIN group men front trench lights co-operated by firing to battery return on communication trench behind HAIRPIN group.	
		4.40 p.m.	Enemy fired on our trenches very heavily from CHOURRIES to the DUMP, with heavy burst mortars.	
		6.0 p.m.	Fired on FOSSE ALLEY & communication with dummy flashes. No. of rounds fired during day 20 "A".	
	18/6/16	10.H15 a.m.	Enemy active on our trenches in G11.6 firing with light field guns from WINGLES, retaliated on likely targets.	
		12.30 p.m.	Enemy fired heavily with field guns & H. 3" from WINGLES on our trenches in G11.6, retaliated on enemy's reserve trenches.	
		6.15 p.m.	Enemy aeroplane flew low over 33rd Division parks found in conjunction with his dummy guns.	

1577 Wt. W10791/1773 500,000 1/15 D. D. & L.   A.D.S.S./Forms/C. 2118.

(10)

Army Form C. 2118.

WAR DIARY
or
INTELLIGENCE SUMMARY.
(Erase heading not required.)

Instructions regarding War Diaries and Intelligence Summaries are contained in F. S. Regs., Part II and the Staff Manual respectively. Title pages will be prepared in manuscript.

Place	Date	Hour	Summary of Events and Information	Remarks and references to Appendices
	18/6/16	9.15 pm	Enemy firing very heavily on our front & communication trenches with light field guns, 4.2" & 5.9", retaliation on enemys trenches	
			N? of rounds fired during day 2H "K"	
	19/6/16	10.15 am	Enemy shelled our trenches in G.11.a & b intermittently for ½ hour, retaliation on trench junction G.12.A.D.2.7½. & G.S.A.6.3.	
		7.30 pm	We blew up a mine near the ruins at G.11.H.P.P.N, collaborated by firing on enemys communication trenches behind the craters.	
		7.10 pm	Enemy shelled our trenches in G.11.A.&b. with 4.2" & light field guns from WINGLES, retaliated on trench junction at G.12.a.2.7½. & communication trench G.S.A.6.3.	
		6.0 pm	Enemy subjected our trenches to G.11.a. to a very heavy trench mortar fire, retaliated at request of infantry +6 "A"	
			N? of rounds fired during day	

(1)

Army Form C. 2118.

WAR DIARY
or
INTELLIGENCE SUMMARY.
(Erase heading not required.)

B/70 Brigade R.F.A.

Instructions regarding War Diaries and Intelligence Summaries are contained in F. S. Regs., Part II. and the Staff Manual respectively. Title pages will be prepared in manuscript.

Place	Date	Hour	Summary of Events and Information	Remarks and references to Appendices
	20/6/16		All quiet on gone till 7.0 p.m. when enemy bombarded our trenches in G.11.A. for two minutes with Right Field guns, retaliated on Loop-hole at G.11.b 8.9. and communication trench at G.5.d.7.2. No of rounds fired during day 8. "A".	
	21/6/16	4.45 pm to 5.0 pm	All quiet on gone till 1.25 pm when enemy shelled HULLUCH ALLEY with 4.2", retaliated on G.5.d.6.2.3. Enemy shelled our trenches in G.11.A. with 77 M.M. and Heavy Trench Mortars, retaliated on G.5.d.2.3. No of rounds fired during day 38 "A".	
	22/6/16		All quiet during morning, but at 9.0 pm; 9.5 + 9.10 pm (previous night) mines were exploded, which caused the enemy to retaliate on G.11.A. + G.4.d, we counterretaliated on by firing on G.S.d.23. and G.11.b.9.7½.	

Army Form C. 2118.

(12)

WAR DIARY
or
INTELLIGENCE SUMMARY.
(Erase heading not required.)

B/70 Brigade R.F.A.

Place	Date	Hour	Summary of Events and Information	Remarks and references to Appendices
	22/6/16	9.15 am	Fired in conjunction with dummy guns.	
		7.50 pm	Enemy shelled out communicated trenches in G.11.b. with (4.2" from WINGLES, retaliated on G.11.b.8.& and G.5.d.6.&.3.	
			Nº of rounds fired 28 "A"	
	23/6/16		All quiet on "zone", fired in conjunction with dummy guns on G.11.a.22.73 + G.11.6.7.97.	
			Nº of rounds fired during day 8 A	
	24/6/16	9.30 am	Some trench mortars & grenades at G.11.b	
		10.45 am	A few ripostes on BORDER REDOUBT.	
		2.48 pm	Some Rifle Grenades in G.11.a + G.11.b	
		5.30 pm	Some trench mortars fell on trenches in G.5.c.	
		7.50 pm	but some were north of ANCHOR SAP. 300 "A"	
			Nº of rounds fired during day	

(13)

Army Form C. 2118.

WAR DIARY
or
INTELLIGENCE SUMMARY.

B/70 Bde R.F.A.

(Erase heading not required.)

Place	Date	Hour	Summary of Events and Information	Remarks and references to Appendices
	25/6/16		Very quiet day.	
		6.7pm	Wire cutting with C/73 Bde at trench junction N of HAIRPIN craters.	
			Fired 12 +E on Machine Gun emplacement at G.11.b.9.7.	
			Nº of rounds fired during day H.O.O "A" 12 A.R.	
	26/6/16		Very quiet day.	
		6.7pm	Wire cutting with C/73 on G.S.a.8.0., a bombardment by us of STEWEL craters and heavy retaliation with trench Mortars & 77 M.M. Guns on G.11.b.	
		8.7pm	Retaliated over HAIRPIN CRATERS at request of infantry for 77.M.M. on G.11.b.	
		10.7pm	Nº of rounds fired during day 113 "A" 8 A.R.	
	27/6/16	3.0 am	Bombards G.12.a. 4.0 to G.12.a.3.5., No support raid by H.L.I. Bde	
		3.40 am	over G.12.d.5.9.	
			Some intermittent 77 M.M. shells on G.11.b. during morning	
			Nº of rounds fired during day 213 "A" 11 A.R.	

1577 Wt. W10791/1773 500,000 1/15 D. D. & L. A.D.S.S./Forms/C. 2118.

(14)

Army Form C. 2118.

B/70 Bde R.F.A.

WAR DIARY
or
INTELLIGENCE SUMMARY.
(Erase heading not required.)

Place	Date	Hour	Summary of Events and Information	Remarks and references to Appendices
	28/6/16		Very quiet during morning	
		12.15 pm	Enemy shelled O BARRY BAY. Nieuch Trench mortars & field guns from O.G.I.	
		2.30 pm	Wire cutting at Sap 104	
		4.0 pm	Wire cutting with section C/73 at G.S.a.8.0.	
		4.0 pm	Fired on Machine gun emplacement at G.11.b.9.7.	
		6.0 pm		
		6.18 pm	We blew up a mine between BOYAU 99 & 98. No of rounds fired during day 170 A 20x 18x+10x7A	
	29/6/16		Very quiet all day. Section C/73 with B/70 carried out cutting at G.S.a.8.0.	
		6.25 pm	Fired on Trench mortar Emplacement at G.12.a.6.6. No of rounds fired during day 316 "A" 29HX	
	30/6/16	1.0 am	4.5" Bde 6.2 cannons carried out raid after explosion of our mine, but were not successful, we bombarded G.S.a.8.0.T machine gun emplacement twice during night of morning	
		2.30 pm	Enemy shelled our trenches on G.11.a. with light	

(15)

B/70 Bole. T.R.F.A.

Army Form C. 2118.

WAR DIARY
or
INTELLIGENCE SUMMARY.
(Erase heading not required.)

Place	Date	Hour	Summary of Events and Information	Remarks and references to Appendices
	30/6/16		Field guns from WINGLES retaliated with C/71 on Machine Gun emplacement at G.11.b.85.95. & G.11.a.60.48.	
		3.0 pm	Wire cutting west of station of C/73 at G.5.d.8.0.	
		5.30 pm		
		8.50 pm	Tried battery salvo on machine gun emplacement for our aeroplanes being fired on.	
		9.3 pm	Two of our minnies sprung south of HAIRPIN CRATERS.	
		9.20 pm	Hostile trench mortar about B.0.4.40.98.	
			N° of rounds fired during day 70 "A" 20 "A X"	

1577 Wt. W10791/1773 500,000 1/15 D. D. & L. A.D.S.S./Forms/C. 2118.

Army Form C. 2118.

WAR DIARY
or
INTELLIGENCE SUMMARY.
(Erase heading not required.)

Instructions regarding War Diaries and Intelligence Summaries are contained in F. S. Regs., Part II. and the Staff Manual respectively. Title pages will be prepared in manuscript.

Place	Date	Hour	Summary of Events and Information	Remarks and references to Appendices

1577 Wt. W10791/1773 500,000 1/15 D. D. & L. A.D.S.S./Forms/C. 2118.

Army Form C. 2118.

WAR DIARY
or
INTELLIGENCE SUMMARY.

70th Bde R.F.A. XV

(Erase heading not required.)

Instructions regarding War Diaries and Intelligence Summaries are contained in F. S. Regs., Part II. and the Staff Manual respectively. Title pages will be prepared in manuscript.

Place	Date	Hour	Summary of Events and Information	Remarks and references to Appendices
Ypernlees	3/6/16		Another artillery quiet. Trench mortars rather active.	
	4/6/16		Another artillery again quiet.	
	5/6/16		Batteries relieved for night. Another evening of our dinner.	
	6/6/16		New battery active. Observers in evening of Right Group.	
			Batteries prepared or about to bring one Officer.	
			B/70 wounded. Reinforcement of Right Group drawn under	
			by Brigade Commander of 92nd Brigade R.F.A.	
			Brigade Head Quarters remained to Detachment.	
Vanquesnes	7/6/16		at Vanquesnes. Brigade Commander relieved of Command	
	8/6/16		15/6/16.	
	to		At Vanquesnes Brigade wagon lines completed under	
	15/6/16		by Brigade Commander.	
	20/6/16			

WAR DIARY

C/70th BRIGADE R. F. A.

June

1916.

Army Form C. 2118.

C/70. R.a. R.n Vol 1

WAR DIARY
INTELLIGENCE SUMMARY.
(Erase heading not required.)

C/70 XV

Place	Date	Hour	Summary of Events and Information	Remarks and references to Appendices
Vermelles	1916 1st June 2nd June		Fired 29 A 87 A* Enemy shelled our front & support trenches at intervals throughout the day. retaliated	mms
			Fired 51 A 109 A* Enemy snipers at our trenches in Rose Trench fire from 3 to 4 am: retaliated at request of infantry (and front)	mms
	3rd "		33 A* Large fire observed at G6 & 84 as result of artillery fire & an explosion took place there at 8.40 pm	mms
	4th "		" 20 A 14 A*	mms
	5th "		No firing	mms
	6th "		Fired 4 A	mms
	7th "		" 20 A 44 A*	mms
	8th "		" 74 A 83 A* :3 4.2 How fired from front in front of DOUVRIN CHURCH in line DOUVRIN — C.10 a 3, 3½	mms
	9th "		22 A	mms
	10th "		" 2 A* Section B/185 relieved reinforcing section C/64 at 7 p.m.	mms
	11th "		" 30 A	mms
	12th "		" 14 A 2 A*	mms
	13th "		" 26 A 30 A* 2nd Lt W.V. Cooly posted to 15th D.A.C. 2nd Lt Wear posted to battery from D.A.C.	mms
	14th "		" 9 A 12 A* Grenade work done on Bogan 99, Anchor Trench & Torso Way, also trench at G 6 c.1.8	mms
	15th "		" 34 A 20 A*	mms
	16th "		" 16 A 27 A*	mms
	17th "		" 9 A 84 A* Zone changed slightly further north. 1 am to 2.30 am — Heavy firing noted on zone	mms
	18th "		" 36 A 44 A* Capt Spinner-Clarke posted to battery. Abnormal T.M activity on Divisional tyre	mms

Army Form C. 2118.

Instructions regarding War Diaries and Intelligence Summaries are contained in F. S. Regs., Part II. and the Staff Manual respectively. Title pages will be prepared in manuscript.

WAR DIARY
or
INTELLIGENCE SUMMARY.
(Erase heading not required.)

Place	Date	Hour	Summary of Events and Information	Remarks and references to Appendices
Vermelles	June 19th	Fired 7A, 8Ax	Quiet Day	MMS
	"20th"	" 11A		MMS
	"21st"	" 14A, 24Ax	5.50 p.m. Mine blown up South of Lettow-nr Crater.	MMS
			4.1 p.m. Mine blown up at G.5.c.4,1½; fired several times at suspected M.G. fmg at aeroplanes; apparently we were silenced at 7.35 p.m. at G.5.c.3,4	
	"22nd"	" 14 A	With the exception of some M.G. fire at aeroplanes, a very quiet day	MMS
	"23rd"	" 2 Ax	Very quiet; no firing on our front throughout the day	MMS
	"24th"	" 20 A & 71 Ax.	First day of Divisional Programme of activity. Fired according to Programme on M.G. Emplacements at G.5.a.9,3. G.inf. 8½,9½ & G.5d.6,7 in first case, not of officers who; the bump kg is at G.5c.5,42 2 direct hits obtained but no actual damage could be seen; no direct hits obtained on other two emplacements.	MMS
			Section salvoes at irregular intervals throughout the night on Russafat Alley	
	"25th"	45 A 72 Ax	Fired at O.P. in G.5.t-11.03 & M.G. in G.5.a.9.3. During night fired salvoes at irregular intervals	MMS
			on Tramway from G.5.d.6½.0½ to G.6.b.4.3	
	"26th"	47 A 49 Ax	Fired on M.G. at G.5.c.9.2; throughout the night on G.5.d.8.5 & G.5.d.9½.2 . L.W. road expected for this night forthcoming.	MMS
	"27th"	89 A 92 Ax	1 a.m. heavy firing with S.O.S. gone, no connection with raid south of Vermelles	MMS

1577 Wt.W10791/1773 500,000 1/15 D. D. & L. A.D.S.S./Forms/C. 2118.

WAR DIARY
INTELLIGENCE SUMMARY.
(Erase heading not required.)

Army Form C. 2118.

Place	Date	Hour	Summary of Events and Information	Remarks and references to Appendices
Vermelles	27th June		(Continued) – Engaged M.G. at G5C 5,6 : fired on Sag Alley during the night.	MMS
	28th	1 a.m.	Battery started firing at Boyau 99 & G5d 0,½ : Guns + Corrected appeared good from O.P.	
		1.10 a.m.	Gas cloud loosed from all our front line trenches from Bordon Redoubt to Hairpin Craters.	
		1.15 a.m.	Trench in front of Quarries apparently on fire, caused by enemy shell.	
		1.20 a.m.	Appreciable increase in our fire; gas cloud very cloudy & appears to move on reaching German trenches	MMS
		1.45 a.m.	Bombing visible N. of Hairpin Craters	
		1.55 a.m.	'Very' lights appear normal, enemy retaliation continuing	
		2.15 a.m.	Fire died down on our front.	
		5.50 a.m.	Our mine blown up; appears to have filled in enemy sap at G5c 9½	
			during the day we fired at O.P. at G5 ± 1,4½ and M.G. at G11b 8½ 9½ : at 8.45 p.m & 11.15 p.m fired two salvos on Croise de Marais	
	29th		Fired 166 A, 148 A + Cut wire at G5c 9,1. Shooting chiefly already. Observation done from Ladadelle Street. Engaged M.G. at G11b 8½,9½. G5a 8,4 & G5c 9½.7	MMS
	30th	1 a.m.	Our mine blown up, signal to begin strafe on G5c & 34, 4½ to G5c 6¾,3½ given by few very lights from Vermelles Water Tower, rapid fire for 5 minutes & then Battery fire 20 sec. During day cut wire	
			(250 A) at G5C 9.1 : two gaps observed 3 and 5 yds wide respectively. Presents chiefly difficult in high G.S.	MMS

[signature]

70th Bde: R.F.A.
Vol: 6
15

H.Q.
15th Divl Arty

Herewith War Diary
for 70th Bde R.F.A
for the month of July
1916. War Diaries of
Batteries detached from
Brigade are attached.

H W Allmitt
Lt Col
Comdg 70th Bde R.F.A.

31/7/16.

Army Form C. 2118

WAR DIARY
70th Bde R.F.A
INTELLIGENCE SUMMARY.

(Erase heading not required.)

Instructions regarding War Diaries and Intelligence Summaries are contained in F. S. Regs., Part II. and the Staff Manual respectively. Title pages will be prepared in manuscript.

Place	Date	Hour	Summary of Events and Information	Remarks and references to Appendices
Field	1/7/16	—	The Brigade remained in Command of 15th D.A. with Hd. Qrs. at Noyelles Chateau. 70th Bde: Batteries distributed between Right & Left Groups 15th D.A. in the following order:— A & D batteries Right Group B & C Left Group. Batteries attached herewith Battery diaries up to & including 23rd July/16.	vol 70 R.F.A
"	11/7/16		The Left Group supported a raid by the 8th Seaforths on enemy trenches in G.4.b. Enemy trenches were entered & occupied by our infantry for half an hour, during which period the Group lifts supported by a traverse of the 39th Div. Arty, fired a gradual & flanking barrage. It is reported that the raid was a very complete one. The infantry have expressed the satisfaction with the support received by our Artillery.	

Army Form C. 2118

WAR DIARY or INTELLIGENCE SUMMARY
70th Bde. R.F.A.

(Erase heading not required.)

Place	Date	Hour	Summary of Events and Information	Remarks and references to Appendices
France	21/4/16		Brigade Commanders held a conference of Left Group & Brigade Commanders of 47th Division. The 5th Divisional Group R.A. was composed of the following Brigades (less one of batteries from the 15th Div. 16th Div. & 170th Bde.) viz: C/70, D/181, C/83, D/44, D/151, which went to upper the 5th Divi. front & upper the CUINCHY SECTOR is support from the 5th Divi. At midnight right section of 70th Bde. Howitzers was out of the line, being relieved in position.	R.
	22/4/16		70th Bde. section upon relief proceeded night march to MONCHY-CAYEAUX. Right Section arrived at MONCHY CAYEAUX.	
	23/4/16		At midnight left Section was out of the line, being relieved by corresponding section of 47th Divl. Artillery. Brigade Commander handed over responsibility for CUINCHY SECTOR over to 94 D.A. Brigade Commander. Staff & left Section of batteries arrived at MONCHY CAYEAUX.	R.
	24/4/16			R.

Army Form C. 2118.

90th Bde WAR DIARY or R.F.A.
INTELLIGENCE SUMMARY.
(Erase heading not required.)

Place	Date	Hour	Summary of Events and Information	Remarks and references to Appendices
Field	25/9/16		At MONCHY CAYEUX.	
	26/9/16		At MONCHY CAYEUX.	
	27/9/16	6.30 am	Left MONCHY CAYEUX & arrived at AUBREMETZ at 1pm.	
	28/9/16	6.45 am	Left AUBREMETZ & arrived at OUTREBOIS at noon.	
	29/9/16	9 am	Left OUTREBOIS & arrived at BOISBERGUES at 10.30 am	
	30/9/16		At BOISBERGUES. Brigade training, open warfare, carried out under Bde: Commander	
	31/9/16	6 am	Left BOISBERGUES & arrived at BOURDON at 1.30 pm	

H W Hllmitt
Lt Col

Ref 1/100,000 Map LENS.　　　　　　　　　　　　　　　　　　Copy No. 6.

No 1

OPERATION ORDERS. No 1

70th Brigade, R.F.A.

25th July 1916.

1. The Brigade will march on 26th July via BEAUVOIS - OEUF - LINZEUX - FILLIERES to AUBREMETz.

2. The Order of march D, C, B & A Batteries, & Head Qrs.

3. The head of the leading battery will be at cross roads 200 yards E of N in ANVIN at 6-39 a.m.

4. Billeting N.C.O's will meet the Billeting Officer at the Chateau MONCHY at 6-30 a.m.

5. Refilling point on 26th July on BRYAS - DIEVAL road just N.E. of BRYAS at 11-0 a.m.

6. Acknowledge.

　　　　　　　　　　　　　　　　　　　　　　　　　Davies Lieut, R.F.A.
　　　　　　　　　　　　　　　　　　　　　　　Adjutant 70th Brigade, R.F.A.

Copy No 1.　　A/70th.
　　　　2.　　B/70th.
　　　　3.　　C/70th.
　　　　4.　　D/70th.
　　　　5.　　File.
　　　　6.　　War Diary.

Ref 1/100,000 Map LENS.
70th Bde R.F.A. No. OO. 2.

Copy No. 6

OPERATION ORDER.

70th Brigade, R.F.A.

26th July 1916.

1. The Brigade will march on 27th July via CONCHY-SUR-CANCHE - VACQUERIE-LE-BOUCQ - AUXI-LE-CHATEUA - WAVANS - OUTREBOIS.

2. The Order of march will be Head Qrs, A, B, C & D Batteries.

3. Starting point Cross roads 400 yards North of C in CANCHE at 7-15 a.m.

4. Billetting N.C.O's will meet the Billeting Officer (Lt. Player) at Brigade Headquarters at 6-0 a.m.

5. Refilling point on 27th inst will be at VACQUERIE-LE-BOUCQ - BOUBERS-SUR-CANCHE Road ¼ mile North of C in VACQUERIE at 11-0 a.m.

6. Please acknowledge.

                           Lieut, R.F.A.
                   Adjutant 70th Brigade, R.F.A.

Copy No. 1.   A/70th.
          2.   B/70th.
          3.   C/70th.
          4.   D/70th.
          5.   File.
          6.   War Diary.

Ref. 1/100,000 Map LENS. Copy No. 6.
70th Bde RFA. No. O.O.3.

OPERATION ORDER.
70th Brigade, R.F.A.

1. The Brigade will march on 29th July to BOISBERQUES.

2. Order of march B, D, C, & A Btys & Hd Qrs.

3. Starting point L of LE QUESNIL FARM at 10-0 A.M.

4. Refilling point on AUXI-LE-CHATEAU - DOULLENS road immediately N.W. of FROHEN-LE-GRAND at 11-0 a.m.

5. Billeting party to meet Lieut. Player at Brigade Headquarters at 8-0 A.M.

6. Please acknowledge.

28/7/1916.

W.J. Davies Lieut, R.F.A.
Adjutant 70th Brigade, R.F.A.

Copy No. 1. A/70th.
        2. B/70th.
        3. C/70th.
        4. D/70th.
        5. File.
        6. War Diary.

Ref 1/100,000 Map LENS.
70th Bde R.F.A. O.O. 4.

5

OPERATION ORDER.
70th Brigade, R.F.A.

1. The Brigade will march on 31st July to BOURDON via HERISSART – first I in ST. HILAIRE – DOMART-EN-PONTHIEU – ST-LEGER-LES-DOMART church – cross roads 300 yds E. of E in BALEUX at OVERS – FRIXECOURT.

2. The order of march C, A, B & D Btys & Hd Qrs.
Brigade starting point 300 yds West of A in AUTHEUX at 6-35 A.M.

3. Divisional starting point junction of 6 roads 300 yds North of 1st L in FIENVILLERS at 7-0 A.M.

4. Billeting party of 1 N.C.O. and 1 gunner per Battery to meet Lieut. Player at Brigade Head Qrs at 5-45 a.m.

5. Refilling point for to-morrow 31st inst on BERNAVILLE – FIENVILLERS Road as to-day, time 7-30 a.m.

6. Please acknowledge.

30th July 1916.

A.J. Davis Lieut. R.F.A.
Adjutant 70th Brigade, R.F.A.

Copy No. 1. A/70th
2. B/70th.
3. C/70th.
4. D/70th.
5. File.
6. War Diary.

War Diary A/70th Bde R.F.A
July 1st — July 29th

July 1st — Shelled approaches and communication trenches in HULLUCH at night.

July 2nd — A busy day. Cut wire at H.13.c.5½.½ (200 rounds A fired). Had 2 guns at Le Rutoire for this purpose. At night shelled roads in HULLUCH. Fired on enemy firing on our planes during the day.

July 3rd — A quiet day

July 4th — At night 10/K.R.I. made a successful raid on Saps 7 and 8 (H.13.c.5½.½). They entered the trenches, destroyed a machine gun & its crew, bombed many dug outs and killed over 30 Germans, & brought back 2 wounded prisoners who belonged to the 5th Bavarians, 4th Bav. Div. 2nd Bav. Corps. We bombarded enemy communication trenches during the attack. The wire was found to be very well cut. (Fired 300 round. A2AX)

July 5th — A quiet day

July 6th — Do. Retaliated for enemy shelling front line at H.7.a.

July 7th — A quiet day. Fired on a working party.

July 8th — Heavy bombardment in the evening on our front system in H.13.c. We retaliated on our night lines and fired 157 rounds.

July 9th — A quiet day

July 10th — Do.

July 11th — Had a 2 minute strafe on H.13.a.3.5½ to H.13.a.5.0 (28 rounds) at 6 pm.

July 12th — 3 2 minute strafes during the afternoon. Fired 32 rounds.

July 13th — A quiet day. Sniped the Bois fontaine — Vendin road at 6.30 pm.

July 18th Quiet day

Quiet day.	July 14th
Do. Fired 26 rounds	July 15th
Quiet day.	July 16th
Fired 50 rounds in retaliation for enemy shelling on front line system in H.23.a.	July 17th
Fired 350 rounds (½A ½A×) on H.29.a 7½.5 to H.29.a.8.4. and H.29.b.0.6 in conjunction with 16th Div. raid at 12.30 a.m.	July 19th *
Fired 300 rounds as above in conjunction with 16th Div raid. The raid last night failed. Tonight it was successful.	July 20th
South African Parliamentary representatives visited the gun position, & the guns were fired for their edification.	July 21st
Quiet day. Right section was withdrawn and marched into Reserve area at Monchy Cayeux. A section of C/77 relieved them.	July 22nd
Left section & Battery H.Q. marched into reserve area & were relieved by C/77 at 11.30 p.m.	July 23rd
Reached Monchy Cayeux after marching all night at midday	July 24th
Rested.	July 25th
Marched to Auxi-le-Château with remainder of Brigade.	July 26th
Marched to Outrebois.	July 27th
Marched to Bonnières.	July 28th
Rested & trained, doing battery gun drill, driving drill & battery staff work.	July 29th

29/7/16

Shirley
Major R.F.A.
Cmdg A/77 Bde

WAR DIARY
or
INTELLIGENCE SUMMARY

D/76" BRIGADE R.F.A.

July 1916

Place	Date	Hour	Summary of Events and Information	Remarks and references to Appendices
Field	3.7.16	8.40a	Enemy shelled Jackdaw Re with 77 M.M. guns	
		9.25a	Enemy shelled Border Redoubt with Trench Mortar	
		11.0am	Enemy shelled Highland Trench very heavily with Trench Mortars & 77 M.M. retaliated in conjunction with C/70 & C/71 on G 5 D 5.4 & G 5 D 4.2	
		11.25a-12.0pm	Enemy fired very heavily on Border Redoubt & Highland Trench with Trench Mortar & bursts of Shrapnel. retaliated on Border Redoubt barrage in conjunction with C/70 & C/71	
		12.45p	Enemy fired on Queen Mary redt. T.M.s	
		3.0pm 4.20pm 6.30p	Dug Cutting at G.5.D.8.0 Our Aeroplanes being shot at retaliated on G5D 7.4 & G.S D.8.4.2	
	4.7.16	8.15a	No M. guns fired during day. 276 A B+A× 77 MM gun fired on Lancer St & Shetwell trench retaliated with C/70 on G5D	
		10-10a	77 M.M. on O.13.1 Highland Trench & Alexander Trench retaliated with C/71 on G5D 5.4 & G 5 D 8.4.2	

WAR DIARY

D/76" BRIGADE R. F. A.

July

1916

From OC D[...]
To HQ 70th Bde.

War Diary – July.

1st ⎫ In action at PHILOSOPHE.
to ⎬ Took part in several small
12th ⎭ bombardments and raids.
The Lone gun had a direct
hit on roof of gunpit on 7th.
No 4 gun was destroyed by a
premature on the night of 8/9th.
One Sgt and one man were
wounded during this period.

12th On night of 12/13th the Battery
HQ moved to waggon line,
RX moved to ANNEQUIN and
was attached to D71
LX stayed at PHILOSOPHE
attached to D72.

Night 22/23 RX came out of action
and marched to MONCHY CAYEUX

Night 23/24 LX & Bty HQ joined RX.
26. Bty marched to MONCHEL
27   to OUTREBOIS
28   to BOMBERGUES

30/7/16   R. A. [signature] RFA
           Capt Comdg D/70.

Army Form C. 2118.

B/70/Bde RHA

WAR DIARY
or
INTELLIGENCE SUMMARY.
(Erase heading not required.)

(1)

Instructions regarding War Diaries and Intelligence Summaries are contained in F. S. Regs., Part II. and the Staff Manual respectively. Title pages will be prepared in manuscript.

Place	Date	Hour	Summary of Events and Information	Remarks and references to Appendices
Field	1.7.Nov.am		Hostile machine gun & rifle directed against our Aircraft retaliated on stations on night line	
		2.0 pm	A few 5.9 " on G.10.C.	
		5.30pm	Trench Mortar active opposite the Guerin, retaliated on night line	
		8.0 pm	Our Aeroplanes heavy fired on	
			No. of Rounds fired during day. 12 AX	
	8.11.16	12.30pm	Wire Cutting at C.5.D.8.0.	
		2.0 pm	Minen went up at Anchor trench	
		3.45am	M.G. & rifle between McEllis & Green Alley	
		6.0 & 6am	Heavy Trench Mortar fires on Clifford St.	
		9.15 pm	Rifle grenades on Kinder Redoubt retaliated on front line & GSD	
		9.35 pm	Burst on Machine Gun emplacement G.11.B.9.7. Junkered German trench	
			at G.11.b.7.4.7. at the following times 10.5 & 10.10pm 10.28 & 10.30pm	
		11.35 & 11.40pm		
			No of Rounds fired during day. 212 A 40 AX	

WAR DIARY
or
INTELLIGENCE SUMMARY

Army Form C. 2118.

(Erase heading not required.)

8/7078ec Bde (2)

Place	Date	Hour	Summary of Events and Information	Remarks and references to Appendices
Field	3.7.16	8.40am	Enemy shelled Sackville Av with 77MM guns	
		9.25am	Enemy shelled Border Redoubt with trench mortars	
		11.10am	Enemy shelled Highland trench very heavily with trench Mortars, 77MM & retaliated in conjunction with C/70 & C/71 on G5D5-4 & G5D6-4.3	
		11.25-31 11.40pm	Enemy fired mg heavily on Border Redoubt & Highland trench with trench Mortor & bursts of Shrapnel. retaliation on Border Redoubt barrage in conjunction with C/70 & C/71	
		12.45pm	Enemy fired on Quarry Bay north T.14.c	
		3.0pm	Dir Cutting at G5 D8.0	
		4.0pm 6.30pm	Enemy aeroplane being shot at retaliates on G5D 8.4 & C G5 D8.42	
	4.7.16	8.15am	No 4 Coy. fired during day. 276 A 84 A X 77MM gun fires on Lancer Lane. Shrapnel trench retaliates with C/70 on G5D	
		10-10am	77MM on O.B.I Highland Trend & Alexander trench retaliates with C/71 on G5 D5-4 & G5 D8-42	

Army Form C. 2118.

WAR DIARY
or
INTELLIGENCE SUMMARY.
(Erase heading not required.)

6/70 Bon R.F.A (3)

Place	Date	Hour	Summary of Events and Information	Remarks and references to Appendices
Field	4.7.16 10.15am 10.25		Fired with C/91 on G5D57y to G5D8-42	
		2.3pm	One of the Wires tapping in C4.B all quiet aftn	
		4.0pm	Wire cutting of C5 D8-0	
		4.50pm	French Motor relief from Baker return to C11B4.7 am and	
		5.12pm	at C.4.D. No of Rounds fired during day 20+A 30AX	
	5-7-16 12.8 am		Our Artillery commenced bombarding Enemy front line	
		12.20 am	Enemy stopped Red Rockets & fired with 77MM guns about	
			order returned	
		12.30 am	Our firing ceased	
		4.0 am	We opening a Mine in Region of Quagmire no Artillery activity	
			during afternoon a few 77MM's in C11B. Retaliated on C5	
			D5-4, C5 D8-42	
		9.30pm	We opening a Mine at C12-13. Informed by own Artillery	
			shelling at Right Bde Zone	
	11-35 (?)		Bombarda at C11B749, 11.30 Gas discharged by us following	
	11-36 pm		by infant bombardment. Enemy guns at Red light. retaliated	
	11-39 pm		by ... 77MM's Arty's on Left Bde Zone	
	11-40pm		enlist 77MM's Arty's on Left Bde Zone	

WAR DIARY
or
INTELLIGENCE SUMMARY.

Army Form C. 2118.

8/7/15 Pt/2

Place	Date	Hour	Summary of Events and Information	Remarks and references to Appendices
Field	5/7/16		No. of Rounds fired during day. S.A.172 AX	
	6/7/16	6 am	Minie went up in G.4 D.3 followed by 77 M.M. shells on Northampton trench. Then all quiet.	
		6.25 am	77 M.M. fires on Sackville trench	
		6.20 am	77 M.M. fires North of Hairpin in G.11.B.	
		6.25 am	Retaliated on G.5 C.3½ × 7½	
		8.30 am	Retaliation on G.5 C.3½ × 7½ for intermittent shelling about Bothés Redoubt with 77 M.M. Gun. All quiet during day. Fired 7.40 pm	
		8.50 pm	Retaliation on G.6 C.0½ 7½ for intermittent shelling of our trench in G.11.B south 77 M.M. Guns.	
			No. of Rounds fired during day. 8 A X	
	7-7-16	6.04 am	Enemy exploded a mine in G.4 B	
		7.15 am	77 M.M. fired on Sackville N. & Highland Trench retaliated on G.5 D7½ 4½	
		9.15	Our Aeroplane taking Photo Hostile Machine Gun & Rifle action	
		10.15 am	Retaliated on Hulpit Line	

WAR DIARY or INTELLIGENCE SUMMARY

Army Form C. 2118.

Place	Date	Hour	Summary of Events and Information	Remarks and references to Appendices
Lille	7-7-16	10.30pm	Retaliation with CNo5 trip shelling Edward on G5D76 4 3 for 20 M.M. gun in Right of Bde Sector.	
		6.40pm	Enemy shelled our front with T.M's all along our Front.	
		7pm	We opened up a wire on C12A in retaliation.	
		7.15pm	Enemy shelled junction of Hulluch Alley & Sherbrooke Trench point 77 M.M. & T.M's. We retaliated on G5D74 4 3	
			No.4 Bomb fired during day. +5AX	
8-7-16	8.30am 8.45am	Enemy fired on Hughlands trench until 77 M.M. retaliation in conjunction with E/70 on G5D7 4.	
		9.50 & 10.30am	Occasional T.M. on Government trench to Gordon Alley and after 77 M.M. about Bryan 95 at 10.30am retaliation with C/71 on G5D 74 4 3	
		10.40am	Retaliated with C/71 on G5D74 4 3 a Shrapnel continues	
		1.20pm	fired an omission of Renfrew on G5D74 4 3	
		7.55pm	barrage 8.40pm 50	
			Snipers established to this barrage owing to Enemy penetrating our Trenches in Right Group Zone	

WAR DIARY or INTELLIGENCE SUMMARY

Army Form C. 2118.

Place: Field
Date: 6/7/16 — 8/7/16

Date	Hour	Summary of Events and Information	Remarks
6/7/16		No. of rounds fired during day. 302 AX	
8/7/16	12.57pm	A few 77 M.M. on Observat. Trench retaliation on G.5.D.23.	
	1.20pm	Enemy fired in Highland Trench with 77 M.M. retaliation on G.5.D.23.	
	4.0pm	Aeroplanes by Aeroplane	
	5.30pm	77 M.M. fired on Hullock Alley Junction behind Quarry	
	5.45pm	77 M.M. fired on Hullock Alley retaliation on G.5.D.23.	
	6.35pm	Enemy shells Alexander & Highland Trench retaliation on G.5.D.23.	
	5.0pm	We blew a mine in H.12.D no retaliation	
	9.45pm	The enemy blew a mine in G.12.D.5-8	
	6.5pm	Enemy fired on Alexander, Highland & Crown trench with	
	6.30pm	4-2", 5-9", at about 100 of the rounds per minute retaliation on G.5.D.23.	
	7.0pm	Fired two salvos on Border Redoubt barrage.	
		No rounds fired during day. 7/A.X.	
10/7/16 &9/7/16	9.0am	77 M.M. fired on G.11-13.B.9 & G.A.B.6.H2 retaliation on G.5.D.32.	
	7.30am	4"-8" on Border Redoubt very heavy fired 500 rounds in	
	10.0am	on Border Redoubt	

1577 Wt. W10791/1773 500,000 1/15 D. D. & L. A.D.S.S./Forms/C. 2118.

B/170 Bde R.F.A.

WAR DIARY
or
INTELLIGENCE SUMMARY.
(Erase heading not required.)

Army Form C. 2118.

(1)

Place	Date	Hour	Summary of Events and Information	Remarks and references to Appendices
Field	10/7/16	2.0 p.m.	Minor spring movement	
	11/7/16		No movements front during day.	
		8.40 a.m.	5.50 & 8.55 a.m. 2 from Krupp fired on our front line on G.11.B. retaliated on G.5.D.74.43	
		9.20 a.m.	T.M.M. fires on G.11.B retaliated on G.5.D.74.43	
		10.30 a.m.	H.21 from Krupp on Algerian Highlanders & French trenches	
		10.45 a.m.	At the rate of one per half minute retaliated in bursts on G.5.D.74.43	
		12.15 p.m. 1.0 p.m.	Our Aeroplane being shot at retaliated on G.5.D.74.43	
		1.0 & 1.8 p.m.	Bombarded G.5.D.2? & G.5.C.23.84	
		1.20 p.m.	2 TM's	
		2.30 p.m.	4 & 25 pm 7 T.M.M. registering between Bryan 98 and the Rhripier retaliated on G.5.D.74.43	
		4.45 & 4.50 pm	Registering continued to Armremond Trench & Sackville & Pitchville on G.5.D.74.43	
		6.0 & 6.15 pm	Bombarded from G.5.C.32.22 & G.5.C.93.3	

WAR DIARY 18/70 Bde RFA (9)
or
INTELLIGENCE SUMMARY.
(Erase heading not required.)

Army Form C. 2118.

Place	Date	Hour	Summary of Events and Information	Remarks and references to Appendices
Field	14.7.16	6.40 am	Enemy shelled our trenches in G.11.A with light field guns retaliated in conjunction with C/70 on G5.D.7.1. No. of rounds fired during day. 27 AX	
	15.7.16	8.50am	77 M/M Guns fired on our French trenches on G5.D.7.1. by request of C/70	
		9.45am	Enemy shelled Quarry Bay with 77 M/M Gun retaliation in conjunction with C/70 on G5.D.7.1.	
		10.30am	77 M/M Guns firing on Quarry Bay retaliated on G5.D.7.1.	
		4.0pm	Fired on damaged O.P. on Machine emplacement at G.11.1387.76. 114 AX 814. No Remarks fired during day.	
	16.7.16	12.0 Noon to 1.0pm	Bombarded Hohenzollern Redoubt & with AX	
		1.0pm to 1.30pm	Wire Cutting at G.5.C.3.3.	
		1.30 to 3.45pm	Bombarded Hohenzollern Redoubt 1 with AX.	
		4.0pm to 12.0 Midnight	fired at intervals on Hohenzollern Redoubt. No. of rounds fired during day. 93A 709 AX	

WAR DIARY or INTELLIGENCE SUMMARY

Army Form C. 2118.

B/70th Bde R.F.A. (10)

Place	Date	Hour	Summary of Events and Information	Remarks and references to Appendices
Field	17/7/16	10 am	Fired at repeated Infantry into G.12 A.4.5. after explosions of Mines on right Bgy of Thiepval.	
		11-25am	We sprung two mines by right Bgy of Thiepval Crater.	
		12.6	Fired 1st rgmt of Infantry in continuation trench behind Crater on G.11.b & G.12.A.	
		3.0pm	Enemy fired on Highland trench with 77mm Gun, retaliated on G.6.D.4.	
		3.30 & 4.30pm	Enemy fired on Iron Way with 77m W/Gun. Retaliated at Expansion with C.F.11 on G.5.D.2m.	
		5.22	Enemy continued to fire on trenches N of Highland trench & Iron Way. Retaliated on G.5.D.3.4.	
		6.20	6.30pm 77 M/M Gun fired on G.11.b.3.4.b. retaliated on G.5.D.2.3.	
		7.15pm	7.25pm Enemy fired with 5.9 on 4.2 on G.11.b.3.4.b retaliated on G.5.D.2.3.	
		8.50pm	77 M/M fired a few rounds on G.11.b.23. Then suddenly opened with heavy bombardment with 5.9, 4.2 & 77mm also heavy T.M.	

B/170 Bde R.F.A.

WAR DIARY
or
INTELLIGENCE SUMMARY.

(11)

(Erase heading not required.)

Army Form C. 2118.

Place	Date	Hour	Summary of Events and Information	Remarks and references to Appendices
Field	1/7/16		Bombardment continued to front & support lines between Border Redoubt & Quarry Copse. Retaliation on G.5.D.33 and on night lines from G.11.B.9.42 to G.5.D.64.3	
		9.0 pm to 9.25pm	fired on Border Redoubt range 115 fuze 15 sec	
		9.25 to 10.6 pm	decreased rate of fire to 20 sec	
		10.10, 10.12 pm	to 30 sec	
		10.30 pm to 10.38 pm	fired on night line from G.11.B.9.42 to G.5.D.64.3	
			at Bty fuze 30 sec	
			No of rounds fired during day 107 A 157 AX	
		12.2 to 7.30, 7.7, 7.17pm	fired on Highland Trench, 7.27 to 7.30 retaliation on G.11.B.7½.9½	
		9.10 am	72 M.M fired on Highland Trench	
		9.50 am	Germans seen on Grass Alley trench on 0.6.B.8.42	
		10.5 am	77 M.M fired on Croix Trench	
		10.35am	fired on enemy observing over parapet at G.6.C.24.92	
		2.0 to 2.30 pm	Registered 9ᵗʰ Companies front line G.5.C.2.3½ to G.5.C.6¾.2¼. Also G.5.C.3¼.5¼ to G.6.C.6.4. Elevating Machine Gun Emplacement	

Army Form C. 2118.

B/10/1941 P.W.O

WAR DIARY
or
INTELLIGENCE SUMMARY.
(Erase heading not required.) (12)

Place	Date	Hour	Summary of Events and Information	Remarks and references to Appendices
Field	16/7/16	3.0 to 3.30 p.m	Heavy bursting of G5 C33.	
		3.30-5.30 pm	Heavy Bombardment on B6, C2 33. G5C33 24 r G5 C 33, 34, G5 C 64	
			Enemy Minnen experienced at Border Redoubt, catapults further Redoubt. Barrage apparently put on supports leading to old Crater.	
			No Rounds fired during day. 150 A 1075 A X	
	17/7/16 after	18 mid to 3.0 am	19 rounds shrapnel and intermittent or burst bursts	
			Heavy from A 29, C 51 O to 6 G 5 C 4 1/2 + Cross front from A 29, C 52, O, C 4, C 54, 14, and occasional rounds on wire at G. 5. C. 33.	
		3.25 to 3.30 am	fired on Border Redoubt at Regiment of Infantry	
		4.15 am	fired in support of Infantry in Crater off Border Redoubt	
		5.35 to 6-3 pm	fired on Border Redoubt	
		6.45 am	fired on Border Redoubt Barrage	

1577 Wt. W10791/1773 500,000 1/15 D. D. & L. A.D.S.S./Forms/C. 2118.

WAR DIARY or INTELLIGENCE SUMMARY

Army Form C. 2118.

(13)

Place	Date	Hour	Summary of Events and Information	Remarks and references to Appendices
Field	19.7.16	7.30am	Fired on Border Redoubt Barrage	
		8.55 am	Enemy shelling our front line in C11b retaliated by registering on O.S.D. 3.3.4. & G5 B53.	
		11.0am to 1.0pm	Bombarded G5C28½ to G5C5½ 2½ & G5C34 5½ & G5C6.4.	
		3.30 to 4.0pm	Wire cutting at G5C3.3.	
		4.0 to 3.50pm	Bombarded as at 12.0 noon.	
		4.25 to 4.40pm	Enemy fired heavily on our trenches in C11b. wait to 2 in & retaliated on C1115 72 9 2	
		6.25pm	Enemy exploded Mine to the right of Kaisern Graben & called barrage, at request of Infantry behind enemy crater.	
		6.45 to 7.20pm	Fired on O.P. at map ref G5 B2.5 at request of Infantry	
			No of Rounds fired during day 79A 740 AX	
	20/7/16 2am		Mine exploded at C4 D82	

B/70 Bde R.F.A.

WAR DIARY
or
INTELLIGENCE SUMMARY.

Army Form C. 2118.

Place	Date	Hour	Summary of Events and Information	Remarks and references to Appendices
Field	20/7/16	6.55am	Our Bties fired in support of Anzacs on C11 B4b.8.	
		10.30am	Enemy fired on O13 & retaliation Bnd with 4.2. retaliated on G11 B7b.9S	
		12.10pm	Enemy fired with 77 MM on to Crown Trench retaliated on G11 B7b.93	
		2.30pm	Enemy fired 4.2's in the Neighbourhood of Crown Trench retaliated on G5D & 4	
		5.19pm	Enemy fired with 77 MM on Highland Trench & OB I retaliated on G11 B7b E	
		at 4.0pm Aerial Bursts were active on Alexandra Trench.	
		5.20 & 5.50pm	fired in support of Anzacs tething Munson Crater	
		No. of Rounds fired during day 4 A 25A X	

15th Divisional Artillery.

70th BRIGADE

ROYAL FIELD ARTILLERY.

AUGUST 1 9 1 6

C O N F I D E N T I A L.

WAR DIARY.

of

70th Brigade R.F.A.

From 1st August, 1916   to   31st August, 1916.

VOLUME Number 14

Major, R.A.

Brigade Major R.A., 15th Divisional Artillery.

H. Qrs
15th DA   HQ 8

Herewith War Diary for
70th Bde RFA for the
month of August 1916

31/8/1916   H W A Christie
                        Lt Col RFA
                 Comdg 70 Bde RFA

15 Jun

Army Form C. 2118

WAR DIARY
or
INTELLIGENCE SUMMARY

90th Bde R.F.A.

Vol 12

(Erase heading not required.)

Place	Date	Hour	Summary of Events and Information	Remarks and references to Appendices
Field	1/9/16		At BOURDON.	
	2/9/16		Lt. 1 BOURDON & arrived at FRECHENCOURT.	
	3/9/16		Lieut. Stores relieved section of the 89th Bde R.F.A. in the line. Battery position being A/90 X.19.d.9.5. B/90.X.19.d.4.5. C/90 X.19.d.1.4. D/90.X.19.d.0.5. Map Area of MARTINPUICH.	
	4/9/16		Brig. Section relieved corresponding section of 89th Bde R.F.A. in the line.	
	5/9/16		At noon Brigade Commander 90th Bde R.F.A. & Staff. relieved Bde Hdqrs & Staff of 89th Bde R.F.A. at LOWER WOOD. There was no wireless trouble during hostilities. The enemy is moving men and ammunition. The valley to the west of MAMETZ WOOD from 10am to 2pm was frequently shelled in S2 & 9c & WELSH ALLEY were heavily shelled with 4.4 m.m. m'2's & 5.9's & ____ 5.9's. The Brigade Observers later on howitzer & 5 other ranks wounded. Hostile shelling has not been so severe during the past 24 hours. in S2. Probably the shells of the enemy the VALLEY west of MAMETZ WOOD has been really shelled whilst m.2's. 4.4.mm were in ordinary. S.9.9.95. The shooting was erratic.	
	6/9/16		Bde observers 20 other ranks wounded - one slightly. Enemy Artillery very active against our trenches in S.2. also along the valley to the West of MAMETZ WOOD. During the evening hostility actively shelled our ammunition ____. ____ l other rank wounded.	
	8/9/16		"A" "C" & "D" Battery position have been shelled throughout the day with m.2's. 5.9's & 9pr. The valley has been heavily shelled. Today all a temporary gun has been in operation on S.2. c.n.d.	

WAR DIARY or INTELLIGENCE SUMMARY

70th Bde R.F.A.

Army Form C. 2118

Place	Date 1916	Hour	Summary of Events and Information	Remarks and references to Appendices
Fricourt	8/9/16 9/9/16	—	Batteries in action. Enemy shelled MAMETZ WOOD with large guns probably 8" at intervals during the morning. All guns in battery of fire. Most damage caused not.	A
	10/9/16		Batteries: Three Horses & four Milken's mostly wounded - Northwards hit. 20th pack horses wounded, one of which plants had to be destroyed. Dugouts in trenches, reinforced with sandbags, used by F.O.O's, & were Turning & low every precaution has been taken; but some of our dug-outs by 40th Bde Battn is not sufficiently low & cleared from the front. B Bn came in so entitled that the presence of the O.P's are not known. The offensive has been continuing throughout.	B
			Enemy shelled batteries' lines around MAMETZ WOOD & the VALLEY. have been shelled at intervals with 77mm's & w.21's. Shrapnel during the day. Also shelled our S.2 & 4.4. INTERMEDIATE TRENCH hundreds of unsuitable damage caused. No real damages caused on any Bde.	C
	11/9/16		Batteries: Both ranks wounded. This morning the enemy shelled MAMETZ WOOD with n.2's & S.9's from h.20 the forwards very heavily on Trenches previously dismantled which light field guns. Ritzmann's trenches were mantled. Attention to our field dug-outs which were investigated were damaged. O.G. I wounded the day. Recruits N.1.	B
	12/9/16		During barrage. Batteries were shelled with 4.4's & great with were shelled during the evening of 19th to evening dem the morning several dumps near overlooking the INTERMEDIATE TRENCH & Kline near the switch LINE Harms M.57 to A few enemy armed Battery Positions - CONTALMAISON & MAMETZ WOOD ROAD were shelled with 5.9's; 7.8" detonation quickly gave.	A

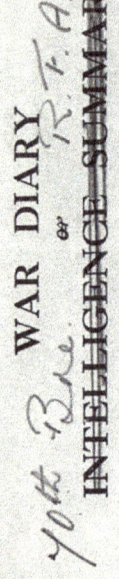

Army Form C. 2118

WAR DIARY
70th Bde R.F.A.
INTELLIGENCE SUMMARY
(Erase heading not required.)

Instructions regarding War Diaries and Intelligence Summaries are contained in F.S. Regs., Part II. and the Staff Manual respectively. Title Pages will be prepared in manuscript.

70th BRIGADE R.F.A.

Place	Date 1916	Hour	Summary of Events and Information	Remarks and references to Appendices
Front	12/8/16	—	During the attack of the Div. on the SWITCH LINE every bit our guns co-operated. Enemy fired gas bursts in bursts, to maintain + 5.9's + H.2.5 on communication trenches, also 8" guns on Road CONTALMAISON- MAMETZ WOOD. Enemy gas bursts 8pm to 9pm all over the valley. Our artillery line had been ordered diminution throughout day with H.2.5. From Midnight to 5am the enemy shelled LOWER WOOD with H.2.5 + 5.9's. Between 2.30am + 4.10am the following were hit:— Lieut. Stuart Johnson + 2 other ranks killed. Casualties Nil.	[initials]
	13/8/16			
	14/8/16		MAMETZ WOOD + LOWER WOOD from 11-30 am to 12 noon were shelled + very heavily with 5.9's + 8". Between the Gun Areas around this battalion + Reserve dugouts in CONTALMAISON Between 6.30pm + 7.30pm were shelled + until 44mm + H.2.5. Casualties Nil.	[initials]
	15/8/16		From 8pm to 3.15am Retaliation was Rassey + MAMETZ WOOD mine Reserve shelled with 5.9's. Positions were held as a quiet day in Reply to all when Retaliation S.O.S. was sent down on S.d + 5.2C was continued until 4.15pm. The shells appeared to harmonise.	[initials]
	16/8/16		EAUCOURT L'ABBAYE + LE SARS, trenches. Positions were unharmed. @ 3pm. Retirement to be an Ammunition dump in the neighbourhood of MARTINPUICH were hit. an Ammunition dump in the new Division SWITCH LINE was hit very great this morning. Tropping being great quiet, + and, by his own side being put on the open, which retaliation. The usual damages were touched out. A/40 firing them retaliating firing. 8pm to 9.30pm with H.2.5 + 5.9's to two trenches which were tense.	[initials]

WAR DIARY or INTELLIGENCE SUMMARY

70th Bde R.F.A.

Army Form C. 2118

Place	Date 1916	Hour	Summary of Events and Information	Remarks and references to Appendices
Field	14/5/16		Casualties: 2nd Lieut Hugh St Pierre Bunbury wounded whilst shaving in his tent (series stile). A/70 position shelled from 1.10pm to 2.15pm with average calibre HE. During the bombardment from 11am to 11pm there were 16 officers. There were seen attempting by snipers whilst his firing. From 5pm to 6pm enemy howitzer & SIXTH AVENUE with HE, M.G.'s & S.G's. The barrage was severed from 7.30pm to 9.30pm many times. Casualties Nil.	
	15/5/16		A/70 position was shelled during the early morning with HE howitzer, a fire was started which was soon extinguished. From 10am to 11:30am a severe hostile barrage turned to the shelter, S.9.'s line just in WELSH ALLEY & SIXTH AVENUE. After our today's attack at less learned, the enemy put a heavy barrage with all kinds of guns up to S.9's on our from this to S.C.B. dumped dealing a number of H.E. & HV fm. sun front into MAMETZ WOOD & also on Rue Fax trench. Wounded to Contalmaison. Casualties: officer Cecil Bunbury Rose Burr slightly wounded total O.R. ranks wounded admitted to hospital 3 others wounded details.	
	16/5/16		This morning the enemy shelled the Indonesville Trench between Road in SKE road in SSO with H.E. & S.9's. During the day of SIXTH AVENUE intermittently shelling during the day of SIXTH AVENUE with S.9.'s HE's & 4.7mm. CONTALMAISON shelled with 8" HV.E from direction of COURCELETTE from 3pm to 3.30pm. Damages to premises with prisoners	

WAR DIARY of 70th Bde R.F.A.
INTELLIGENCE SUMMARY

Army Form C. 2118

70th BRIGADE R.F.A.

Place	Date 1916	Hour	Summary of Events and Information	Remarks and references to Appendices
Fricourt	20/8/16		Casualties — 20th Bde ranks wounded (Hospital). At 7.30 am our infantry left High Wood working in the direction of Tank Tail (S3.d.1.64) They advanced to the consolidating enemy trench Trench from direction S3.b.8.2 to S3.b.2.8. At 8.30 am a heavy hostile barrage from direction of LESARS, of m/c + 5.9s in our front trench system this was reported from 10.30 am to 11.30 am the hostile trench has been dug behind the Switch line S3.a.6.8. At 2.45 pm our infantry attacked from S3 b 2.7 to S3.b.1.6½ to western end of High Wood + captured the switch line (S3.d.1.6½) from M33.d.0.n. to M33.c.0.0. The enemy retired towards MARTINPUICH. Our batteries with good observation. Divisional programme + B/ barrage carried out.	
	21/8/16		Casualties 10th ranks died by Shr. Gas 10th ranks killed by Steel. 20th ranks wounded (Hospital) 20th ranks wounded (Duty) During the whole of last night really this morning the enemy shelled Bazentin-le-Petit + see Brigade battery positions with gas shells + "tear shells" lasting from 10 pm to 5 am. was very intense. Hostile shelling approx B/ B/ chiefly directed from the LE SARS district. D/40 received was a very unsuccessful bombardments of enemy works + lines + number of direct hits delivering considerable damage.	
	22/8/16		Casualties Nil. During the night calm, morning the enemy open red fire B/	

Army Form C. 2118

WAR DIARY
70th Bde R.F.A
INTELLIGENCE SUMMARY
(Erase heading not required.)

Place	Date 1916	Hour	Summary of Events and Information	Remarks and references to Appendices
Field	22/9/16		Clear, humid, with rest freedom as on the nights of the 20th/21st Aug. During the morning our front has been very quiet. At 1.30pm enemy shelled S.16.c. with H.2's & 4 pm S.9.a. with 5.9's, from COURCELETTE at the will of Fired every two minutes. Div. Barrage carried out. P.barrative N.1.	
	23/9/16		Enemy Artillery moderately active, but there has been no particular concentration or bombardment to record. Hostiles aeroplanes have been particularly active during at B day. Barrage carried out at intervals with batteries of Battery Section of 250th Bde R.F.A. relieving somewhere batteries the 70th Bde. P.A upon relief the proceeded to FRECHENCOURT.	
	24/9/16		At 5.15am enemy shelled S.9.a.Y.T. continuing the bombardment until 7.30am with 5.9's & 4.2's from direction of LE SARS — At 9.10am to 10am they shelled BAZENTIN-LE-PETIT WOOD with H.2's. The remainder of the day two been fairly quiet. Rear Section of every hue moved out with staff P. 250 Bde R.F.A. relieved ear Section of 70th Bde in the afternoon the relief, 70th Bde War Section proceeded to FRECHENCOURT.	
	25/9/16		Brigade Commander & Staff proceeded to FRECHENCOURT. 70th Bde to remain at FRECHENCOURT in rest for several days	

Army Form C. 2118

WAR DIARY
70th Bde or R.F.A.
INTELLIGENCE SUMMARY
(Erase heading not required.)

Instructions regarding War Diaries and Intelligence Summaries are contained in F.S. Regs., Part II. and the Staff Manual respectively. Title Pages will be prepared in manuscript.

Place	Date	Hour	Summary of Events and Information	Remarks and references to Appendices
Field	26/8/16 to 31/8/16		Bde at FRECHENCOURT.	R/

W.S.A Clarke Lieut Col
Comndg 70th Bde R.F.A

SECRET. Copy No. 6

Ref 1/100,000 Map AMIENS. + Albert combined sheet 1/40,000
O.O. No. 7.

OPERATION ORDER.
70th Brigade, R.F.A.

1. Remaining sections of 70th Brigade will march to-morrow to the wagon lines of leading sections, & thence to the gun lines. Sections will be relieved in the gun line between 3 a.m. and 4 a.m.

2. Lieut. McCorquodale will command rear sections.

3. Starting point Cross roads 200 yards West of B in BETHENCOURT at 1-15 p.m.

4. Route as laid down in preliminary orders.

5. 200 yards to be left in rear of each battery.

6. Refilling point same as for today D.7.d. at 7 a.m.

7. Please acknowledge.

                                        Lieut, R.F.A.
                              Adjutant 70th Brigade, R.F.A.

Copy No. 1.   A/70th.
        2.   B/70th.
        3.   C/70th.
        4.   D/70th.
        5.   File.
        6.   War Diary.

Ref Maps LENS & AMIENS 1/100,000 & ALBERT, combined sheet 1/40,000
70th Bde No. O.O. 6.

Copy 6

OPERATION ORDER.
70th Brigade, R.F.A.

1. Battery Commanders will carry out a reconnaissance to-morrow with the Brigade Commander.

2. A Motor bus will pick up these officers at BOURDON CHURCH at 6-30 A.M.

3. These officers will meet the Brigade Major at junction of roads E.3.d.7.7. (ALBERT combined sheet).

4. <u>Points to be noted</u> :-
   (a) Water supply at gun and wagon lines.
   (b) Route to be followed during relief.
   (c) Hours at which German barrages are put on.
   (d) Hours for watering.
   (e) No of rounds at dump at guns.

5. The 19th Division will leave down all wires, ammunition at guns, maps etc.

6. On completion of reconnaissance a motor bus will convey officers to their new billets.

7. During the reconnaissance officers are not to go about in groups.

8. 70th Brigade take their own guns into action.

9. Please acknowledge

1st August 1916.

Lieut. R.F.A.
Adjutant 70th Brigade, R.F.A.

Copy No. 1. A/70th.
       2. B/70th.
       3. C/70th.
       4. D/70th.
       5. File.
       6. War diary.

Copy No. 5

SECRET.
70th Bde No. O.O. 5 (a)
Ref 1/100,000 Map LENS - AMIENS.

OPERATION ORDER.
70th Brigade, R.F.A.

1. The Brigade will march to-morrow under Lieut. Davies to FRECHENCOURT, via VIGNACOURT - FLESSELLES - VILLERS BOCAGE - MOLLIENS- AU- BOIS- MONTIGNY.

2. Starting point an order of march as detailed on preliminary order.

3. Refilling point as on 1st August.

4. Billeting N.C.O's to meet Billeting Officer at the Church, BOURDON at 4-45 A.M.

5. Please acknowledge.

                           Lieut, R.F.A.
                   Adjutant 70th Brigade, R.F.A.

Copy No. 1.   A/70th.
        2.   B/70th.
        3.   C/70th.
        4.   D/70th.
        5.   File.
        6.   War Diary.

70th Brigade R.F.A.   For information.

Preliminary Orders in connection with the relief of the 19th D.A. by the 15th D.A.
         (N.B. These orders are liable to amendment).

1.   The 15th D.A. will relive the 19th D.A. on the nights of 3rd/4th and 4th/5th August. Relief to be complete by 6.0 a.m. on August 5th.

2.   One section of each battery will go into the line on the night of 3rd/4th. The remaining sections on the night of 4th/5th

3.   Units of the 19th Divisional Artillery will march back via Main road in CATERPILLAR VALLEY - MATETZ - BECORDEL E.16.a. E.15.a. thence cross country to main AMIENS road.
        Units of the 15th Divisional Artillery will march up via BAISIEUX - HENENCOURT - MILLENCOURT - ALBERT - BECOURT - LOZENGE WOOD (X.27.b.5.0.) - FRICOURT and thence dry weather track East of MAMETZ WOOD.

4.   The B.G., R.A. wishes Brigade Commanders and Battery Commanders to carry out a reconnaisance tomorrow (2nd inst) a motor bus will be at BETHENCOURT Church at 6 a.m. tomorrow morning to pick up officers of 71st and 73rd Brigades. From there it will proceed to BOURDEN Church when it will probably arrive about 6-20 a.m. to pick up officers of 70th and 72nd Brigades.
        Officers will meet the B.M., 15th D.A. at junction of roads E.3.b.7.7. (ALBERT Combined sheet)
        The motor bus will proceed from BOURDON by the road which runs along the left bank of the SOMME to AMIENS, thence by the main AMIENS - ALBERT road.

5.   Points on which Brigade and Battery Commanders should satisfy themselves during the reconnaisance are :-
(i)   Water supply (both at gun position and wagon lines)
(ii) Route to be followed during relief.
(iii) Hours at which the different German barrages are generally put on.
(iv) Hours for watering horses.
(v)   Number of rounds in the dump at the gun positions.

6.   Batteries of the 19th D.A. (i) will leave down all telephone wire
                                        which is on the ground.
                                   (ii) will leave behind all the ammunition
                                        dumped at the gun position.
                                   (iii) will leave all maps, etc as per usual
                                        which may be of use to batteries of 15th
                                        D.A.

7.   When the B.M. 15th D.A. meets Brigade and Battery Commanders tomorrow at E.3.b.7.7. he will inform them of the Brigade of the 19th DA. which are being relieved by Brigades of the 15th D.A.

8.   On completion of the reconnaisance the motor bus will convey officers of the 15th D.A. back to their new billets. The senior officer will inform all officers of the hour at which the bus will start.

9.   During the reconnaisance officers of the 15th D.A. are not to go about in groups.

10.   15th D.A. will go into the line with their own guns.

1.8.1916.   (sd)   E. Boyce   Major, R.A.
                        Brigade Major, 15th Divisional Artillery.

Ref. Maps LENS-AMIENS 1/100,000 and ALBERT Combined sheet 1/40,000.

15th D.A. Operation Order No. 31.

2.8.1916.

1. With reference to the relief of the 19th D.A. by the 15th D.A. The instructions contained in the Preliminary Orders issued on 1st instant hold good with the exception of para 10.

2. The 15th D.A. will take over the guns of the 19th D.A. (including those in the workshops and under repairs and on indent) and will hand their own over to the 19th D.A.

The guns of the 15th D.A. will be handed over at their present gun parks.

Gun stores (including dial sights) will be similarly taken and handed over.

3. One section of each Battery also Headquarters, Nos 1 and 2 Sections "A" Echelon, and "B" Echelon D.A.C. will march to-morrow in accordance with attached March Tables.

The sections of each Brigade will march under the orders of the senior Officer of the Brigade going forward tomorrow, the Brigades being independent of one another.

Guides for these sections will be at railway crossing W.27.d.7.3. at 5 p.m.

The Sections of the D.A.C. will march under the orders of the Section Commanders independently of one another.

Each section of the D.A.C. will send a small party forward to reconnoitre the position it is to occupy and to send back guides.

4. All units of the 15th D.A. will march with their full complement of ammunition.

5. Sections of the 15th D.A. will relive sections of the 19th D.A. between 2 a.m. and 4 a.m. on the 4th instant, unless otherwise ordered.

6. Each Brigade will send two signallers to report to 2/Lieut WHITE, R.E. tomorrow morning at 8 a.m. at D.A., H.Q. for duty at the Advanced Telephone Exchange. These men will continue to be rationed by their Brigade.

(sd) E. Boyce   Major, R.A.,
Brigade Major, R.A., 15th Divisional Artillery.

March table for 3rd August to accompany 15th D.A. O.O. No. 31.

Unit in order of march.	From.	to.	Route.	Starting point.	Time.	Remarks.
One section per battery 70th Bde.	FRECHENCOURT.	Wagon lines of batteries of 19th D.A. being relieved in E.6.d. North of the road.	ROUTE. As laid down in preliminary orders.	Cross roads 200 yards west of B in BEHENCOURT.	1-38 pm	200 yards to be left in rear of each Bty or Brigade.

WAR DIARY

C/70th BRIGADE R. F. A.

September

1916

C.R. 31.

To. H.Q
  XV D.A

Herewith war-diary of
70th Brigade R.F.A. for
month of September.

   H W Allgood(?)
        Lt Col. R.F.A.
Comdg 70th Brigade R.F.A

CONFIDENTIAL.

War Diary

of

70th Brigade Royal Field Arty

From 1st September, 1916 to 30th September, 1916.

Volume Number 15

[signature]

Major, R.A.

Bde Major 15th Divisional Arty.

Army Form C. 2118

WAR DIARY
7th Bde or D.F.A.
INTELLIGENCE SUMMARY
(Erase heading not required.)

SECRET

Instructions regarding War Diaries and Intelligence Summaries are contained in F.S. Regs., Part II. and the Staff Manual respectively. Title Pages will be prepared in manuscript.

Place	Date	Hour	Summary of Events and Information	Remarks and references to Appendices
	4/9/16		Enemy shelled our front and support trenches from S.2.c S.3.d with light field guns in 3.1.c and 5.4.c from 3.15 p.m. to 4 p.m. 3 hrs was afterwards very quiet during the afternoon.	W.E.M.
	5/9/16		Casualties in S3c and S4d kept up from time to time. All quiet on Brigade front. One O.R. wounded.	W.E.M.
	6/9/16		Barrage on yesterday. Situation on own artillery fire. 1 O.R. wounded by own artillery fire	W.E.M.
	7/9/16		The front Division attacked between 4 & 5 a.m. High Wood at 6 p.m. 70 Bde Inf AD 5 a.m. & the attack was intended to carry out a advance on our Bde right and line. High Wood was taken. Bn Inf troops have moved on our front and b...	W.E.M

1875 Wt. W593/826 1,000,000 4/15 J.B.C. & A. A.D.S.S./Forms/C. 2118.

SECRET

Army Form C. 2118

Instructions regarding War Diaries and Intelligence Summaries are contained in F. S. Regs, Part II. and the Staff Manual respectively. Title Pages will be prepared in manuscript.

WAR DIARY
70th In Bde ~~of~~ R.F.A.
INTELLIGENCE SUMMARY

(Erase heading not required.)

Place	Date	Hour	Summary of Events and Information	Remarks and references to Appendices
	8/9/16		Fairly quiet on Bde front. Battery on S.3.c and S.1.b kept up a slow rate of fire in the afternoon 5.9's and 4.2's and slight hostile gunning where our own current in S.2.d.	W.E.M.
	9/9/16		The 1st Division made the attack at 2 pm to N of Bois (15th Div) attacked High Wood. S.W. corner our own batts attacked 70th Bde barrage S.2.c and S.2.d and W.2.d.W. attack was a failure. Great artillery along the whole line all day	W.E.M.
	10/9/16		Divisional area changed to S.1.d 37.4 on the right to MUNSTER ALLEY on the left. F and 4 brought road in M.3.c and location in S.2.b and S.30 during the day. Intermittent shelling on S.30 and S.H.C Enemy put up a barrage on S.30 and S.H.C at 10 & 35 pm & 7 pm. Infantry from direction of Sicart in S.6.a & S.3.	W.E.M.

1875 Wt. W593/826 1,000,000 4/15 J.B.C. & A. A.D.S.S./Forms/C. 2118.

SECRET

Army Form C. 2118

WAR DIARY or INTELLIGENCE SUMMARY

70 Bde R.F.A.

(Erase heading not required.)

Instructions regarding War Diaries and Intelligence Summaries are contained in F.S. Regs, Part II. and the Staff Manual respectively. Title Pages will be prepared in manuscript.

Place	Date	Hour	Summary of Events and Information	Remarks and references to Appendices
	11/9/16		70 Bde R.F.A. moved the whole Brigade from horses on 10 K to wagon on the 11 K at which time the Brigade orders reached the Left Divisional Group. D/70 completed the move to the 73rd Bde R.F.A. which they relieved on the 10th July 15 noon. Except for intermittent shelling by light field guns showing no great damage. 1. O. B. Bombarded by our artillery the 5.9 howitzer fall in the afternoon.	W.E.M.
	12/9/16		Slow bombardment of Bottom trench carried out from 6.30am to 6.30pm. Enemy shelled Bazentin le Petit wood from 5.15 to 6.15 pm with 5 guns from the direction of Flers.	W.E.M.
	13/9/16		Nothing to report — enemy quiet day. No great counter-battery bombardment of Martinpuich.	W.E.M.
	14/9/16		Barrage on trench and Wood Lane and Wood Lane continued, consisted of Martinpuich and 43.Z. Today fully lent Second dawn on Flers. Hostile artillery concentrated by our artillery — Think our artillery supremacy ≈ hollow with	W.E.M.

SECRET

Army Form C. 2118

WAR DIARY or INTELLIGENCE SUMMARY

70th Bde or RFA

(Erase heading not required.)

Instructions regarding War Diaries and Intelligence Summaries are contained in F. S. Regs., Part II. and the Staff Manual respectively. Title Pages will be prepared in manuscript.

Place	Date	Hour	Summary of Events and Information	Remarks and references to Appendices
	15/9/16		6 a.m. Barrage been opened out on a prearranged plan by 70 Bde. & Divisional Artillery point of attack being high ground North East of Martinpuich. At 6.20 a.m. the infantry attacked and difficulty all Boche trenches down on the objective. 6.30 a.m. Enemy were within 100 yards of registration of infantry. Our heavy guns replying heavily. Tak Bomb'd & well covered. Tanks. At 9-35 a.m. enemy opened a heavy B.a barrage along our line in SAA. 10.5 a.m. from Bois Labe. Enemy attended to B by our artillery. A & B by our infantry. 12-20 pm. More 7th heavy guns silenced. occupied the remainder of Martinpuich. 12.30 p.m. Boche retiring all day. 5.30 on SS3 on heavily shelled at 6.30 pm. 10.7 then shelled a heavy fire on our front lines, which covered on and off through the night. Bayeul fired from 9 pm 2 5 am south.	W.E.M.

SECRET

70th Bde or RFA

WAR DIARY
INTELLIGENCE SUMMARY
(Erase heading not required.)

Army Form C. 2118

Place	Date	Hour	Summary of Events and Information	Remarks and references to Appendices
	15/9/16		Hostile artillery very active on our front. Heavy shelling in S & E. MARTINPUICH throughout the day. Much transport seen on MARTINPUICH - BAPAUME Road also on LIGNY - BOUDLENCOURT road. Enemy seen to be holding 2nd line trench off of Sap.	W.E.M.
	17/9/16		Hostile artillery was active on the infantry front & as there was a heavy mist no balloons could go up. [illegible] at 5.30 pm the hostiles opened up with heavy shell in MARTINPUICH direction, shelling our guns on BAPAUME - [illegible] road. A/71 moved up into a new position near BAZENTIN-LE-PETIT in S 2 b 1.1 5	W.E.M.
	18/9/16		Our guns were very active. 2/Lt N.W. Duff 52 & Capt Wood, 70th Avenue Battery, 51 and Major H.V. Siddle and 5 O.R. [illegible] other ranks were shelled with gas of all calibre and Montauban [illegible] wounded by shell fire. 1 O.R wounded	W.E.M.
	19/9/16		6 in. artillery active throughout. The day. Heavy heavy [illegible] Stafford Trench at 3.30 pm Enemy much or which was shelled	W.E.M.

SECRET

WAR DIARY
70th Bde or R.F.A
INTELLIGENCE SUMMARY

(Erase heading not required.)

Army Form C. 2118

Place	Date	Hour	Summary of Events and Information	Remarks and references to Appendices
	20/9/16		Enemy artillery active on MARTINPUICH, HIGH WOOD, and Sch. mostly 81-210 and 77mm guns used. Capt. Jamieson R.A.M.C. attacked P.U.O. went sick with P.U.O. C/171 and A/71 relieved by C/170 and B/170.	WEM
	21/9/16		Enemy registered M.34.d. with 8.210 and 77mm gun. Our Alley, just south of our Brigade H.Q. at about c/14.8.9? — 7th Armoured Div was in action along with B/170 and continued during the morning.	WEM
	22/9/16		8.10 mm up into a new position S of MARTINPUICH and HIGH WOOD were shelled continuously during the morning by 8.210 and 77mm guns. O in C Bequeroult d'ABBAYE	WEM
	23/9/16		Enemy shelled SWITCH LINE with 8.210 and slight bursts of fire during the morning. M 31.a c c and St Some 8.210 shelling M 35.c and St heavy from Shelling and Le Barque. The Field guns fired from within EAUCOURT-L'ABBAYE and a high velocity gun from P.Y.S. During the afternoon a Field gun fired on M 35.c, M 33 and M 34. A 77mm gun shelled BAZENTIN LE PETIT all through the night. At 11 p.m. we bombarded M.3.a.8.9½ and M.3.c.7.3 to 7.0 which was bombarded meanwhile.	WEM

SECRET

Army Form C. 2118

Instructions regarding War Diaries and Intelligence Summaries are contained in F.S. Regs., Part II. and the Staff Manual respectively. Title Pages will be prepared in manuscript.

WAR DIARY
70th Bde of RFA
INTELLIGENCE SUMMARY
(Erase heading not required.)

Place	Date	Hour	Summary of Events and Information	Remarks and references to Appendices
	24/7/16		Enemy shelled MARTINPUICH at intervals during the day from WARLANCOURT with 5.9" and 8.3". Hostile artillery were also active on 23rd and 24th. 70th Bde H.Q. moved up into new Headquarters in BAZENTIN-LE-PETIT (S8 c 7.3). A/70 also went into a new position by the other.	WEM
	25/7/16		S.V. enemy shelled all along the front with 5.9" of irregular intervals. At 12:30 p.m. enemy bombarded M27 a 6.8 and heavily. He seemed to be shooting from GEUDECOURT & de TRANSLOY. During the night BAZENTIN-LE-PETIT and round round about were shelled with gas shells and 8.3".	WEM
	26/7/16		During the morning hostile artillery was very quiet. RFA 1385 when she put up a barrage in retaliation to our barrage. Infantry attacked on whole front of our front. were successful. BAZENTIN-LE-PETIT was shelled all day. A/70 during the day and night. C/70 and Killed Major G.E. KIDD. through wounding Lieuts S.B.C.CAPPER and G.NAIRN. 2nd Lt. CAPPER shown wounds of shown. A.A.Lt. S.O.R. Cooper wounded by shell fire.	WEM

SECRET

Army Form C. 2118

Instructions regarding War Diaries and Intelligence Summaries are contained in F.S. Regs., Part II. and the Staff Manual respectively. Title Pages will be prepared in manuscript.

WAR DIARY or INTELLIGENCE SUMMARY

70 Bde P.F.A.

(Erase heading not required.)

Place	Date	Hour	Summary of Events and Information	Remarks and references to Appendices
	27/9/16		Enemy shelled HIGH WOOD, PRUE TRENCH and MILL RIDGE at intervals during the day with 5.9, 4.2 and 7m.m. MARTINPUICH was also heavily shelled. Very quiet night. 70th Bde fired a barrage from W.E.M. M.9/5.3 to M.9.A.3.1 2nd/Lt C.E. FISKE attached to A/70. Captain G.A. BRIGGS 2nd/Lt WILKINS to B/70 2nd Lt R.C. LORIMER to B/70	W.E.M.
	28/9/16		3 other Bdes were from TCD [?] [?] Enemy artillery was again very active & shelled the whole of our own front intermittently. 3 h.e. guns seemed to be shooting from de BANQUE and T HILLOY on & MILLENY wood also enemy intermediates [?] the village of S.A.R.S. and the Farm in M.9.14 the FIERS [?] reported. 1 O.R. wounded by enemy artillery 2nd/Lt I.A.W. GRANT posted to A/70	W.E.M.

SECRET.

Army Form C. 2118

WAR DIARY
70th Bde or RFA
INTELLIGENCE SUMMARY
(Erase heading not required.)

Place	Date	Hour	Summary of Events and Information	Remarks and references to Appendices
In the field	29.9 -16		The daytime was quiet, but all batteries were firing throughout the night. During the daytime inspections.	RMP
	30.9 16		Batteries registered trenches in M21 & M15 & Faucourt l'Abbé, and shelled parties of Germans walking from Faucourt l'Abbé to Le Barque.	RMP

W Stelwick
Z. Col RFA
Comdg 70th Brigade RFA

WAR DIARY
70th Bde or R.F.A.
INTELLIGENCE SUMMARY
(Erase heading not required.)

SECRET

Army Form C. 2118

VOL 13

Place	Date	Hour	Summary of Events and Information	Remarks and references to Appendices
Field	1/9/16		Brigade at rest in FRECHENCOURT finishing action relieved previous night of 10th and 73rd Bdes	W.E.M.
	2/9/16		70th Bde H.Q. relieved from 71st Bde H.Q. Remaining sections of batteries relieved sections of 71st and 73rd Bde batteries	
			A/70 relieved from B/71 Battery, positioned at 57.5.2.3.0	
			B/70 " " A/73 " "	
			C/70 " " B/73 " " " 57.0.2.8.5	W.E.M.
			D/70 " " C " "	
			D/70 " " D " " 57.2.0.8.3	
			Group under 70th Bde H.Q. consisted of A/70, C/70, D/70 and D/70	
			71st Brigade H.Q. taken over from 71st Bde were in a dug-out at 57.2.0.0.6	
			5.3.a and 5.3.d from 11 to 11·30 am enemy barraged our trenches with 5.9.2 and 5 a.c. attacked High Wood at 10·30 am by 1st Div - S and S.W. of the front We barraged part of S.W. and A - 15 he front Division was unable to hold any ground. Nothing in 5.3.d and 5.1.a very slight enemy shelling.	W.E.M.
	3/9/16			

SECRET

B/70 Bde R.F.A.

Army Form C. 2118.

WAR DIARY
or
INTELLIGENCE SUMMARY.
(Erase heading not required.)

B/70

Instructions regarding War Diaries and Intelligence Summaries are contained in F. S. Regs., Part II. and the Staff Manual respectively. Title pages will be prepared in manuscript.

Place	Date	Hour	Summary of Events and Information	Remarks and references to Appendices
In The Field	2/9/16	6	Relieved A/72nd Bde R.F.A. at their Gun Position S.20.b.	GO22
	3/9/16	noon	Attack by Infantry of 1st Division in HIGH WOOD. supported.	GO22
			N° of rounds fired during day 697 "A" 24 AX	GO22
	4/9/16		Attack by Infantry of 1st Division in HIGH WOOD. supported.	GO22
			N° of rounds fired during day 820 "A" 340 "AX"	GO22
	8/9/16		Attack by Infantry of 1st Division in HIGH WOOD supported	GO22
			N° of rounds fired since 4/9/16 1230 "A" 910 "AX"	GO22
	10/9/16		Relieved by A/251 Bde R.F.A.	GO22
	11/9/16		Relieved A/251 at their position in X.14.d.	GO22
	12,13/9/16		Relieved A/235 Bde RFA at their gun position in X.23.b.	GO22
	15/9/16		Supported 15th Division attack on MARTINPUICH	GO22
			N° of rounds fired since 8/9/16 4102 A 2153 AX	GO22
	16/9/16		Moved battery position forward to X.12.a.	GO22
			Relieved by A/104 Bde RFA	GO22
	19-20/16		Relieved A/71 Bde R.F.A. at their Gun Position S.8.b.1½.b.	GO22
	"		N° of rounds fired since 15/9/16 1644 "A" 1210 "AX" GO22	GO22

G.O.B. Danbery
Major
Comd: B/70 Bde R.F.A.

1577 Wt. W10791/1773 500,000 1/15 D. D. & L. A.D.S.S./Forms/C. 2118.

WAR DIARY or INTELLIGENCE SUMMARY

Army Form C. 2118

Place	Date	Hour	Summary of Events and Information	Remarks and references to Appendices
FRECHENCOURT	September 1		Right section left FRECHENCOURT 2 p.m. Arrived wagon lines 8:30 p.m.	MMS
	2		Left section ditto. R.F section took over from B/73 RFA at 8 a.m.	MMS
MALBORO' WOOD (CATERPILLAR VALLEY)	3		Left section took over from B/73 left section at 8 a.m. At 12 noon, 1st Division attacked HIGH WOOD. Other attacks could be observed to DELVILLE WOOD. Heavy fighting on right from direction of GINCHY. Battery fired in conjunction with 1st Div. attack on S.3.b. German counter-attacked. About 5 p.m. and retook what they had lost. Fired 409 A 82 Ax	MMS
	4		Continuous barrage kept up on trenches in S.3.b. Fired 867 A 327 Ax	MMS
	5		Fired 274 A 199 Ax ⎱ Barrage at intervals day & night on S.3.b. to demolish, and prevent ⎰ repair of British line though this square	MMS
	6		Fired 229 A 220 Ax	MMS
	7		Fired 263 A 208 Ax	MMS
	8		Fired 222 A 151 Ax Further attack by High Wood by 1st Dn. Again the success was only temporary	MMS
	9		Fired 756 A 380 Ax Barrage in conjunction with attack on HIGH WOOD at 5:30 p.m. Firing kept up till late.	MMS
	10		Fired 792 A 634 Ax Rt section moved out to take over from B/252 RFA behind Contalmaison. S.O.S. on 1st Div. front in afternoon. Barrage kept up till night.	MMS
	11		Left section relieved remaining section of B/252 RFA at 10 a.m. At 12 noon battery moved into position in CONTALMAISON at X.17.c.2.6. Fired 542 A 240 Ax	MMS

SECRET

Army Form C. 2118

Instructions regarding War Diaries and Intelligence Summaries are contained in F.S. Regs., Part II. and the Staff Manual respectively. Title Pages will be prepared in manuscript.

WAR DIARY
or
INTELLIGENCE SUMMARY
(Erase heading not required.)

6/70

Place	Date	Hour	Summary of Events and Information	Remarks and references to Appendices
CONTALMAISON	September 12		Fired 257 A 259 Ax	MMS
	13		" 275 A 268 Ax	MMS
	14		" 364 A 368 Ax Telephone lines laid out in preparation for operations on 15th. Our reserves very active on MARTINPUICH. A great deal of aeroplane work. One aeroplane brought down a balloon in flames about 6 pm. Enemy put up an intense barrage on S 7 a about 7.15 pm; lasted about 15 minutes. Firing seemed to come from direction of AUCOURT L'ABBAYE.	MMS
CONTALMAISON VILLA	15		Fired 678 A 728 Ax Barrage opened at 5.20 am, when infantry attacked MARTINPUICH in conjunction with operations of other divisions on both flanks. Previous to the several "TANKS" advanced over the enemy trenches on our front. Intense barrage kept up for 40 minutes, creeping back to Ref 150 yds in front of infantry as they advanced. Firing diminished at 9.20 am. Received orders to move battery forward. Left the position at 11 am; marched up the road through CONTALMAISON to position at X 11 d 8,9½. Laid out lines of fire & registered new lines.	MMS
	16		Fired 207 A 150 Ax	
	17		" 323 A 143 Ax Observed from trench in H 31 C ; registered Le Sars.	MMS
	18		" 245 A 70 Ax	MMS
	19		" 126 A 124 Bx	MMS
	20		" 210 A 125 Ax	MMS

J. Bray
Captain
Comdg C/70 Bde RFA

WAR DIARY.

D/70" BRIGADE R. F. A.

October

1916

C O N F I D E N T I A L.

War Diary

of

70 Bde RFA

1st October, 1916.   to   31st October, 1916.

VOLUME. 16

[signature]

Major R.A.

Brigade Major 15th Divisional Arty.

Army Form C. 2118.

VOL.14

WAR DIARY
of
INTELLIGENCE SUMMARY   Volume 16.
(Erase heading not required.)

Instructions regarding War Diaries and Intelligence Summaries are contained in F.S. Regs., Part II. and the Staff Manual respectively. Title Pages will be prepared in manuscript.

Place	Date	Hour	Summary of Events and Information	Remarks and references to Appendices
BAZENTIN LE PETIT	Oct.16 1		Supported 23rd division attack on LE SARS.	JfS
	2		First sections of Batteries moved out to rest.	JfS
	3		H.Q. A B and C Batteries relieved by 71st Bde. R.G.A. and go into rest at ST GRATIEN.	JfS
ST GRATIEN	4 to 16		A, B, C, Batterys and H.Q. in rest at ST GRATIEN. D Batty in action in front of MARTINPUICH (attached to 73rd Bde R.G.A.)	JfS
CONTALMAISON VILLA	17		70th Bde R.G.A. relieves 71st Bde R.G.A. A,B, and C Batteries behind MARTINPUICH.	JfS
	18		Division on our right attacked at 3.40 am. Our batteries put up barrages as ordered to support them.	JfS
	19		D/70 Taken over at 7.0 am. A quiet day. Usual night barrages.	JfS
	20		Usual night barrage. LOUPART WOOD bombarded by How. Batteries with SF shell at 2 am.	JfS
	21		at 12.6 the Brigade bombarded LITTLE WOOD for ten minutes in conjunction with attack by 9th division. LOUPART WOOD bombarded at 2 am for five minutes.	JfS
	22		D/70 bombarded LITTLE WOOD at 5.0 am for 3 minutes. A B and C Batteries swept ground behind LITTLE WOOD.	JfS
	23		All guns bombarded GALLWITZ TRENCH for five minutes at 5.30 am.	JfS

WAR DIARY or INTELLIGENCE SUMMARY

Army Form C. 2118.

Place	Date	Hour	Summary of Events and Information	Remarks and references to Appendices
CONTALMAISON VILLA	Oct. 24.		D/70 bombarded M.G. emplacement at 11.0 am and 3.30 pm and houses from 2. – 3. pm.	JJS
	25.		At 11. am & 3 pm creeping barrage returned to drive enemy out of shell holes in front of GALWITZ TRENCH. One How. of D/70 fired 10 rds an hour on W. corner of LOUPART WOOD on account of ^enemy activity there.	JJS
	26.		2.30 pm A & B Batteries strafed WARLANCOURT for 3 mins. From 2.30–3 pm D/70 strafed gun emplacement, and at 3.45 pm strafed a suspected single gun position at M.4.c.5.3½.	JJS
	27.		At 2.0 pm a party of about 100 infantry moving in extended order S of west end of LOUPART WOOD were dispersed by our fire. Tracks in M.10.c. suspected gun positions in M.4.c. and LITTLE WOOD were searched during the day.	JJS
	28.		Several parties of enemy were fired on with good effect all W of LOUPART WOOD to GREVILLERS TRENCH. GALWITZ TRENCH kept under fire all day, numerous direct hits being registered.	JJS

WAR DIARY or INTELLIGENCE SUMMARY

Army Form C. 2118.

(Erase heading not required.)

Place	Date	Hour	Summary of Events and Information	Remarks and references to Appendices
CONTALMAISON	29	7.45 a.m.	Enemy ration party seen on road N of BUTTE WOOD were fired on and dispersed.	JB
			During the morning fire was kept at a slow rate on GALWITZ TRENCH, GALWITZ BUTTE and tracks running N. towards LOUPART WOOD with occasional bursts of fire.	
		3.30 p.m.	Our artillery barraged the line N of the BUTTE and then the whole of the enemy's front.	JB
	30th	8.30 a.m.	Ration party emerging from LOUPART WOOD were fired on & dispersed.	JB
	31st	2.30 a.m.	False S.O.S. alarm.	JB
		12.30–5 a.m.	Night area search carried out every half hour	
		8 p.m.	Night area search repeated.	

W J Chick
Lieut Col. R.G.A.
Comndg 70th Bde R.G.A.

Army Form C. 2118.

D/70

WAR DIARY
or
INTELLIGENCE SUMMARY
(Erase heading not required.)

Instructions regarding War Diaries and Intelligence Summaries are contained in F. S. Regs., Part II. and the Staff Manual respectively. Title Pages will be prepared in manuscript.

Place	Date	Hour	Summary of Events and Information	Remarks and references to Appendices
MARTINPUICH	Oct. 16.		Came into action W of MARTINPUCH.	JJS (copy)
	4.		Registered on LE SARS trenches.	JJS
	5.		Day & night Barrages carried out as ordered. Nothing to report	JJS
	6.		23rd Division took LE SARS. Battery fired in trenches in M.15.a.	JJS
	7.		Barrage M.10.C.6½.6. – M.10.d.0.5	JJS
	8.		Day & night barrages fired as ordered. Nothing to report	JJS
	9.		Day barrage on M.9.C.9.5. to M.9.d.6.5	JJS
	10.		Day & night barrage as ordered. Nothing to report	JJS
	11.		Fired on dump in M.16.C.6.4.	JJS
	12.		Barrages as ordered. Nothing to report.	JJS
	13.		Barrage on M.10.d.4.3½ to M.10.d.0.5	JJS
	14.		Barrages as ordered. Nothing to report.	JJS
	15.		Barrage by day on M.9.d.5.6. to M.9.C.9½.5. By night on M.10.d.3½.3½	JJS
	16.		to M.10.C.9.5½	JJS
	17.		Barrage by day M.10.d.4½.3½ to 0.4.3.4 and M.10.C.15 to d.9.5½	JJS

WAR DIARY
INTELLIGENCE SUMMARY

(Erase heading not required.)

Army Form C. 2118.

Place	Date	Hour	Summary of Events and Information	Remarks and references to Appendices
MARTINPUICH	Oct/16 18	7am	Taken over by 70th Bde R.F.A.	(SS Copy)
			(Signed) R. FREER	
			Capt. R.F.A.	
			Commdg D/70 Bde R.F.A.	

CONFIDENTIAL.

War Diary.

of

70th Bde R.F.A.

From 1st November, 1916 - 30th November, 1916.

VOLUME 17.

1.11.16.

[signature] Captain,

for Bd Major 15th Divisional Arty.

CONFIDENTIAL.   CR 93

Head. Qrs
15th Divl Arty

Herewith War Diary for 70th
Bde R.F.A. for the month of
November 1916.
  Volume No. 17.

30/11/16

H W A Christie
Lt. Col. RFA
Comdg 70th Bde RFA

CONFIDENTIAL

VOLUME 17, SHEET 1

Vol 15

Army Form C. 2118.

WAR DIARY
or
INTELLIGENCE SUMMARY

(Erase heading not required.)

Instructions regarding War Diaries and Intelligence Summaries are contained in F.S. Regs, Part II. and the Staff Manual respectively. Title Pages will be prepared in manuscript.

Place	Date	Hour	Summary of Events and Information	Remarks and references to Appendices
(CONTALMAISON VILLA)	Nov. 16.			
	1.	7.30am.	A few men seen in the open S. of LOUPART WOOD were dispersed by our fire.	JfS
		3.40pm	S.O.S. Barrage fired in accordance with orders received. All appeared normal on our front.	JfS
			During the night we fired at RAVINE in M4 & j, trench junction at M9 a & GALLWITZ SWITCH & wire in M9a.	
	2.	8.10am	Working party on road in M4 were shelled & dispersed.	JfS
	3.	11.am	Party walking along Sunken road in M4 b 59 were dispersed by our fire.	
		11.30am	Party of enemy at G34a were driven back into LOUPART WOOD by our fire.	JfS
		2.10pm	Two large columns of white smoke seen to rise from about H34d. 50th D.A. onwards command of Left Group.	
	4.		GALLWITZ TRENCH shelled during the day.	JfS
		1.15pm	GIRD LINE barraged. Very quiet night.	
	5.	11.0am	Work at trench junction in M9a was stopped by our shelling.	JfS
		2-4pm	Several parties of the enemy proceeding from COURCELETTE towards BAPAUME, also parties in M4 C & a were fired on with good effect.	
		7am	We kept the day quiet. In M4 continual movement for which considerable barrage fire was observed. The relief in the trenches in front of LITTLE WOOD, the relieving party being observed to run back.	
	6.		Division on our right attacked. The enemy's barrages were started too late to catch our men advancing across the open. Parties seen at M[?]787 were dispersed. Posts at M9d 70 q 5 were shelled and the enemy driven out three times in the day.	JfS

2449 Wt. W14957/M90 750,000 1/16 J.B.C. & A. Forms/C.2118/12.

CONFIDENTIAL
VOLUME IV
SHEET II

WAR DIARY or INTELLIGENCE SUMMARY

Army Form C. 2118.

(Erase heading not required.)

Place	Date	Hour	Summary of Events and Information	Remarks and references to Appendices
CONTALMAISON VILLA.	Nov 16. 6 (cont)	9 a.m.	Enemy were observed entering a house in M11a which was shelled by the Hows. 2 direct hits were obtained. Caravan 30-40 Germans to bolt out along the road where they were dispersed by our search along the road. Small parties were fired on during the day. Several casualties being observed. GALWITZ LINE shelled also part - front of Wm M9d. Working parties in GREVILLERS LINE were dispersed with several casualties. About 20 men entered house in M11c 86 which was shelled. The party returned to wood. Several small parties were fired on & dispersed.	JB
	7			JB
	8			JB
	9	2.15 p.m.	A party shelled a wrecked aeroplane near M3a77 in spite of our fire. Wire in M10c & M9d also strong point in M9a were shelled. Observation very difficult owing to mist. A pigeon was seen at X11 or 5? flying north at about 1.30 p.m. Observation conditions very bad owing to low lying mist.	JB
	10			JB
	11			JB
	12	8.30 a.m.	30-40 enemy standing to in front of LITTLE WOOD were shelled and dispersed, many casualties being observed. O.P.s at M10c.14 and working party at M9a55 shelled. Movement in GALWITZ LINE was stopped by our fire.	JB JB

CONFIDENTIAL
VOLUME 17
Sheet III

Army Form C. 2118.

WAR DIARY
or
INTELLIGENCE SUMMARY
(Erase heading not required.)

Place	Date	Hour	Summary of Events and Information	Remarks and references to Appendices
CONTALMAISON VILLA	Nov.16 13"		During the afternoon a heavy mist made observation impossible so a heavy barrage was kept up on our night barrage line.	JH
	14"		Several small parties seen in COUPE GUEULE were fired on with good effect. Also parties at E of LOUPART WOOD. A suspected anti-tank gun in M.4.b. was fired on. During the afternoon a hostile aeroplane flew over our batteries absolutely unhindered at a very low altitude. A few hours later A & C batteries were shelled heavily with 8" Hows. from the direction of GREVILLERS.	JH
	15" 3.0pm		We fired on a party seen moving in front of LITTLE WOOD causing a few casualties. Also parties seen on main road at COUPE GUEULE. Parties of Germans seen along GREVILLERS LINE in M.4. were dispersed by our fire.	JH
	16" 12.30pm		We bombarded wire in front of trench in M.4.a.5.4. causing much damage for 40 x on each side of this point.	JH

CONFIDENTIAL
VOLUME 17
SHEET IV

Army Form C. 2118.

WAR DIARY
or
INTELLIGENCE SUMMARY
(Erase heading not required.)

Place	Date	Hour	Summary of Events and Information	Remarks and references to Appendices
CONTALMAISON VILLA	Nov.16 17.		During the day movement was observed in M9d35 and stopped by our fire.	JFS
	18.	12.2?pm	2 men entered trench in M9a23 which was shelled causing much smoke for about 5 minutes.	JFS
	19		During the day we shelled parties of men walking on the main road in COUPEVELLE with good effect. Registration was carried out on the BUTTE de WARLENCOURT and new S.O.S. line.	JFS
	20.	10.am 2.0pm	First Section of Batteries relieved by Sections of 72 Bde. R.F.A. Parties of Germans on main road in COUPEVELLE were fired on & several casualties caused.	JFS
PIERREGOT	21 22nd to 30th	2.30pm 12 noon	Relief by 72nd Bde R.F.A. completed H.Q A,B & C Batteries in rest at PIERREGOT. D Battery in action in MARTINPUICH.	JFS JFS

M.W.A Christie
Lt Col RFA
Comdg 70th Bde RFA

2449 Wt. W14957/M90 750,000 1/16 J.B.C. & A. Forms/C.2118/12.

C O N F I D E N T I A L

WAR DIARY

of

70th Brigade R. F. A.

from 1st December, 1916 to 31st December, 1916.

VOLUME 12

Major, R.A.
Brigade Major 15th Divisional Artillery.

SECRET

Army Form C. 2118.

WAR DIARY
or
INTELLIGENCE SUMMARY.

70 Brigade Royal Field Artillery

Vol 16

(Erase heading not required.)

Instructions regarding War Diaries and Intelligence Summaries are contained in F. S. Regs., Part II. and the Staff Manual respectively. Title pages will be prepared in manuscript.

70th BRIGADE

Place	Date	Hour	Summary of Events and Information	Remarks and references to Appendices
Field	December 1916 5th		Brigade in rest at PIERREGOT 1-3 spent in reorganization.	RuS
"	6th		First sections moved up to line.	RuS
"	7th		Remainder of batteries moved up.	RuS
"	8th		H.Q. moved up and took over from 71st Brigade. (D/73 came to 70th Brigade C/70 was broken up)	RuS
"	9th		5 O.P.S. shell by them not an Infant Bosch in the evening. HQ at BAZENTIN LE PETIT	RuS
"	10th		Fired several times during the day on parties round LITTLE WOOD	RuS
"	11th		Roads and tracks in vicinity of WARLANCOURT shelled at dusk	RuS
"	13th		Lt. Col Christie went to hospital. Major D Awbrey took over command of Brigade	RuS
"	14th		H Q in LOUPART WOOD shelled with 5.9's in the early morning	RuS
"	15th		Enemy fired several times to work a GREVILLERS LINE.	RuS
"	16th		Co ordination scheme registration	RuS
"	17th		Registration of his zones	RuS
"	18th		Observation impossible and I think must be [illegible]	RuS
"	19th		Tracks in vicinity of WARLANCOURT shelled	RuS
"	20th		Much aerial activity, no our planes brought down by gun fire	RuS
"	21st		Think must [illegible] of undue importable	RuS

SECRET

WAR DIARY
70th Brigade R.F.A. Vol 18
INTELLIGENCE SUMMARY

Army Form C. 2118.

Place	Date	Hour	Summary of Events and Information	Remarks and references to Appendices
Field	December 1916			
"	22nd		Tanks went into wood shells during the night	Rlns C
"	23rd		Area search from GALLWITZ to REVILLERS LINE Enemy not reported	Rlns C
"	24th		Short bursts on Nature and of WARLENCOURT all night	Rlns C
"	25th		Frozen forward lines & Patches in Mud Much.	Rlns C
"	26th		Occasional improved during the stillday	Rlns C
"	27th		Day — off LITTLE WOOD nearly stultify storm.	Rlns C
"	28th		Batt. Concentration commenced 2pm	Rlns C
"	29th		LittleWood concentration at 11am & 2pm.	Rlns C
"	30th		A/71 heavy shelled by 8" from 10am to 3pm heavy enter shells in his	Rly 5
"	31st		MARTINPUICH shelled intermittently also Bazuta — Martinpuich road.	Rlns 5

G B Davidson
Major R G A
Commanding 70thRFA Brigade RFA

Army Form C. 2118.

WAR DIARY
INTELLIGENCE SUMMARY
(Erase heading not required.)

Page I
"C" Battery
70th Brigade RFA

Place	Date	Hour	Summary of Events and Information	Remarks and references to Appendices
MARTIN PUICH	1916 Dec 22nd		72nd Bde. RFA assumed Tactical control of the Battery	SBS
	Dec 23rd		71st Bde. RFA assumed Tactical control of the Battery	SBS
	Dec 29th		Capt. S.D. GRAHAM, M.C. from 532 Bty RFA assumed command of the Battery vice Capt. R.E. Kane, M.C. who assumed the duties of 2nd in command. During the above period the Battery Zone was M17a43 to M17a06. Reference	SBS
	Dec 31st		Map. LIGNY THILLOY 1/20000. An average of 320 rounds per day were fired by the Battery. The Battery position was at S3C7575	SBS

P.S. Graham
Major RFA
Commanding 70th Brigade RFA

Confidential.

War Diary

of

70th Brigade R. F. A.
_____

1st January 1917 - 31st January 1917.

VOLUME 19

Major, R.A.

Brigade Major 15th Divisional Artillery.

SECRET

Army Form C. 2118.

Vol 19   Vol 17

WAR DIARY
or
INTELLIGENCE SUMMARY
(Erase heading not required.)

Instructions regarding War Diaries and Intelligence Summaries are contained in F.S. Regs., Part II. and the Staff Manual respectively. Title Pages will be prepared in manuscript.

Place	Date	Hour	Summary of Events and Information	Remarks and references to Appendices
BAZENTIN - LE PETIT	Jan/17 1st		GALLWITZ LINE was shelled throughout the day. Barrage fire was kept up on the GALLWITZ LINE during the night.	JBS
	2nd		GALLWITZ LINE was bombarded during the day and a barrage kept on the night. The enemy shelled MARTINPUICH & the BAZENTIN - HIGH WOOD road with 4.2's & 5.9. Observation led one to think min	JBS
	3rd		Movement seen on the BAPAUME ROAD was shelled & several parties dispersed.	JBS
	4th		During the day the GALLWITZ LINE was shelled.	JBS
	5th		was fired at with some success. Movement in COUPE GUEULE Observation led one to think. GALLWITZ LINE shelled and several	JBS
	6th		working parties are reported to have been scattered.	JBS
	7th		Relief of A&C/70 relieved by A & B/72. Relief by 72nd Bde. R.F.A. completed.	JBS
PIERREGOT	8th to 16th		Hd.Qrs. A/70 & C/70 in rest at PIERREGOT	JBS

SECRET   Army Form C. 2118.

WAR DIARY
or
INTELLIGENCE SUMMARY
(Erase heading not required.)

Vol 19

Place	Date	Hour	Summary of Events and Information	Remarks and references to Appendices
BAZENTIN - LE - PETIT	Jan/17 16.			
	17.	2.30/m	Half A/70 and C/70 relieved half of A/72 & B/72. All batteries bombarded CAMP TRENCH, movement was observed in M5a and one gun switched on.	ffs
		5.10, 6.30, 7.45 pm, 4.30, 5.45, 6.am bursts of fire on DRY DITCH, tracks & dump W. of LITTLE WOOD.		
	18.		Working parties on the GALLWITZ TRENCH were shelled during the morning with great success. 2.15 pm bombarded M4 a.14 & M30l 74qt. Our two nightly bursts of fire on obtel in M4d.	ff
	19.	10.30 am	All batteries bombarded M4 a 66 to M3 & 80.75. A party of men seen in M3 & were fired on & dispersed.	ffs
		5 to 6.35 pm	All Batteries carried out a bombardment in conjunction with III Corps H.A. Howitzers bombarded Trench junctions and GREVILLERS LINE. Observation very difficult owing to mist. Enemy artillery very active during the day.	ffs

2449 Wt. W14957/M90 750,000 1/16 J.B.C. & A. Forms/C.2118/12.

SECRET

Vol 19

Army Form C. 2118.

WAR DIARY
or
INTELLIGENCE SUMMARY

(Erase heading not required.)

Place: BAZENTIN-LE-PETIT

Date	Hour	Summary of Events and Information	Remarks and references to Appendices
Jan/17 20	11 am.	All batteries bombarded CAMP TRENCH and during the day M.G's & Dugouts in M10 c & d.	JS
	3 p.m.	GALLWITZ LINE and DRY DITCH searched. Working party at M4 & 87 was fired on & dispersed. During the night 18 pdrs searched by 100's to 500 x behind the front line. Observation poor.	
21		During the day bursts of fire on approaches in front system. How's fired on Dump at W end of LITTLE WOOD and Dug outs in the vicinity. Observation very poor.	JS
22		During the day bursts of fire on the enemy front system & communications. A small working party at M3 d 88 was dispersed. How's bombarded suspected T.M., O.P. and M.G. during the day. Observation bad, owing to ground mist.	JS

SECRET

Army Form C. 2118.

WAR DIARY
or
INTELLIGENCE SUMMARY Vol 19
(Erase heading not required.)

Place: BAZENTIN - LE - PETIT

Date	Hour	Summary of Events and Information	Remarks and references to Appendices
Jan/17 23rd	1 pm	Wire cutting at M10c06 & M9d15 was carried out during the day & these points were shelled in conjunction with our M.G's during the night. Have engaged starting point at M9c3525 – 7 direct hits been obtained. Also suspected M.G.s & O.P.s. A red coloured enemy plane was brought down by one of ours at M19b.	JBS
24	65	Wire cutting was carried out at M9d15 & M10c06. These points being kept under fire during the night. Our M.G.'s fired 18 hrs fired on front line. Harrassed suspected(?) M.G.'s and O.P.'s. Much aerial activity - two enemy planes being brought down. Thick mist during the morning & evening but middle of day was clear & observation good.	JBS

SECRET

WAR DIARY
or
INTELLIGENCE SUMMARY Vol 19
(Erase heading not required.)

Army Form C. 2118.

Place: GRAZENTIN LE PETIT

Date	Hour	Summary of Events and Information	Remarks and references to Appendices
Jan/17 25		Wire cutting during the day and gaps in wire kept under fire during the night.	JFS
26"		Wire cutting during the day and considerable aerial activity. Observation poor.	
27"		Wire cutting during the day and gaps kept under fire at intervals during the night. During the afternoon parties of enemy were seen & fired on during the day movement at GREVILLERS LINE and GREVILLERS STRONGPOINT was fired on and wire cutting carried out. During the night the gaps in the wire and M3d and M4d were searched for 500 yards.	JFS
28"	3pm	All batteries opened fire & front line and searched N in the zone. Heavitgen bombarded suspected M.G.s	JFS
		During the night for 18 mins Jordan gaps in wire - known bombarded same M.G.s only day.	JFS

2449 Wt. W14957/M90 750,000 1/16 J.B.C. & A. Forms/C.2118/12.

SECRET

Army Form C. 2118.

WAR DIARY or **INTELLIGENCE SUMMARY** Vol. 19

(Erase heading not required.)

Instructions regarding War Diaries and Intelligence Summaries are contained in F.S. Regs., Part II. and the Staff Manual respectively. Title Pages will be prepared in manuscript.

Place	Date	Hour	Summary of Events and Information	Remarks and references to Appendices
BRENTIN LE [?]	Jan/17			
	26th 3.30pm		18pdrs searched Nr. Starting for SOS* on GALWITZ trench. Hun fired during the night 18pdrs	JS
			kept the saps in wire under fire.	
	30th 1.45am		8/10 GORDONS raided the BUTTE. 18pdrs a/ tour took part, the former taking the left of the creeping barrage and the latter bombarding H.Q.s and M.G.s The raid was a complete success and little enemy	JS
	Jan 18		barrage was very poor and slow in appearing.	
	8.15 am		Huns bombarded Gomp and GAUNDT trenches.	
	5.20pm		18 pdrs opened fire on their S.O.S lines & searched immediately SOS* hr SOS*. Observation very poor during the day	JS

2449 Wt. W14957/M90 750,000 1/16 J.B.C. & A. Forms/C.2118/12.

SECRET

WAR DIARY
or
INTELLIGENCE SUMMARY

Army Form C. 2118.

Vol 19

Place	Date	Hour	Summary of Events and Information	Remarks and references to Appendices
GUEZENTIN LE PETIT	Jan/17 31st		Early — this morning the Batt'n 14.9's — 26" AVENUE were heavily shelled with 5.9's from the direction of LE BARQUE. GALLWITZ LINE was bombarded during the day.	JB1

R.J.Bolton
Major R.J.A.
Commdg. 70th Bde. R.J.A.

SECRET

Army Form C. 2118.

WAR DIARY

INTELLIGENCE SUMMARY. B/70 Bde. R.F.A.

(Erase heading not required.)

Instructions regarding War Diaries and Intelligence Summaries are contained in F. S. Regs., Part II, and the Staff Manual respectively. Title pages will be prepared in manuscript.

Place	Date	Hour	Summary of Events and Information	Remarks and references to Appendices
Field	6/1/17	10.30am	Bombarded CAMP TRENCH with 72 rounds	
		2.15pm	Bombarded GALWITZ ZONE. Enemy shelled M.27.C + M.26.D at intervals with 77.7A.M Guns	
			No of rounds fired during day 136 A. 285 MX	S.O.S.
	7/1/17		Searched the ground in M.G.C. nothing to report	
			No of rounds fired during day 131/A 286 MX	S.O.S.
	8/1/17		Fired into LOUPART TRENCH, P/S ROAD, + ACHIET TRENCH	
			No of rounds fired during day 82 A. 257 MX	S.O.S.
	9/1/17		Carried out Bombardments as ordered by Brigade	
			No of rounds fired during day 70 A. 270 MX	S.O.S.
	10/1/17		Searched the enemys trenches and tracks carrying out programme as ordered by Bde	
			No of rounds fired during day 30 A. 160 MX	S.O.S.
	11/1/17		Slight Bombardments of Enemys front line Enemy Bombarded and Sprinkled M.17 + M.24 very heavily at intervals during the day	
			No of rounds fired during day 10 A. 158 MX	S.O.S.

G.B.Barker
Comdg B/70Bde R.F.A.
Major

SECRET

WAR DIARY

INTELLIGENCE SUMMARY. B/70 Bde R.F.A

(Erase heading not required.)

Army Form C. 2118.

Place	Date	Hour	Summary of Events and Information	Remarks and references to Appendices
	12/1/17		Fired on enemy's front line at intervals as ordered by Brigade. Enemy Artillery very quiet. No of rounds fired during day 30 "A" 60 "AX".	9P.
	13/1/17		Fired in accordance with Brigade Programme. Enemy shelled our trenches during the day in GILBERT ALLEY O.G.I, LE-SARS, and the valley between SEVEN ELMS + PRUE COPSE. No of rounds fired during day 40 "A" 162 "AX"	9P.
	14/1/17		Fired on northern side of ACHIET TRENCH in G.34.C, also fired and dispersed enemy's working party. Enemy shelled LE SARS, EAUCOURT L. ABBAYE, + RUTHERFORD ALLEN. No of rounds fired during day 100 "A" 360 "AX"	9P.
	15/1/17		Fired into LOUPART TRENCH in G.34.C + PYS ROAD in G.33.b. Carried out programme as ordered by Bde. Enemy shelled EAUCOURT-LE-ABBAYE + EAUCOURT ROAD	

S.P.B.Barker Major
Comdg B/70 Bde R.F.A

SECRET

Army Form C. 2118.

WAR DIARY
or
INTELLIGENCE SUMMARY. B/70 Bde R.F.A.

(Erase heading not required.)

Instructions regarding War Diaries and Intelligence Summaries are contained in F.S. Regs., Part II. and the Staff Manual respectively. Title pages will be prepared in manuscript.

Place	Date	Hour	Summary of Events and Information	Remarks and references to Appendices
	15/1/17		No of rounds fired during day 20 "A" 30 "AX"	90
	16/1/17		RUTHERFORD AVENUE nr M.26 was shelled during day also ENCOURT-L-ABBAYE. Fired on enemy's front line at intervals as ordered by Bde. No. of rounds fired during day — A 230 "X"	SOS SOS
	17/1/17		Rejoined 70th Bde.	

S.O.B Rawlins Major
Comdg B/70 Bde R.F.A.

WAR DIARY or INTELLIGENCE SUMMARY

Army Form C. 2118.

C/70 Bde RFA

Place	Date	Hour	Summary of Events and Information	Remarks and references to Appendices
S30 15	1917			
	Jan 1st to Jan 6th		C/70 Bde RFA remained under Tactical control of 71st Bde R.F.A., covering the same zone -	R.F.
	Jan 5	9.30 am	At 2.30 p.m. the Battery was shelled with 8" from direction of GREVILLERS. 52, 8" shell were fired into the Battery. Two guns and two dugouts were destroyed. The Battery men suffered no casualties.	R.F
	Jan 6	12 noon	B/72 Bde relieved C/70 Bde who proceeded to rest area at PIERREGOT.	R.F
	Jan 16	11.15 am	Right Half Battery C/70 relieved right half B/72 in same position.	R.F
	Jan 17	12 noon	Relief completed. Bty under tactical control of 72nd 71st	R.F
			Bde RFA. Bty under tactical control of 72nd Bde RFA	R.F
	Jan 22nd	12 noon	Bty placed under tactical control of 72nd Bde RFA	R.F
			Zone altered to M116b75 to M10d35.00.	
	Jan 30	1.45 am	2.15 am Bty fired barrage in support of a raid by the 44th Inf Bde on the BUTTE and QUARRY. Raid successful. 20 prisoners taken.	R.F

P. S. Graham
Major RFA
Comdg C/70 Bde RFA

CONFIDENTIAL

W A R   D I A R Y.

OF

70th. BRIGADE R.F.A.   15th. DIVISIONAL ARTILLERY

for month of February 1917.

VOLUME XX

Brig: General.

Commanding 15th. Divisional Artillery.

WAR DIARY
or INTELLIGENCE SUMMARY

70 Bde R.F. Vol 20 Vf/18

Army Form C. 2118.

Place	Date	Hour	Summary of Events and Information	Remarks and references to Appendices
BRAZENTIN LE PETIT	Feb/17 1st	12 noon to 5 pm	Salvoes were fired in GALLWITZ TRENCH and on tracks leading to it and again during the night.	
		4.45 to 4.48 pm	All batteries bombarded CAMP TRENCH	JBs
	2nd		Movement on tracks was seen of parties on during the day.	
		12 noon to 5 pm and 7am to 8am	batteries fired on dry ditch, CAMP, GALLWITZ and GREVILLERS TRENCHES.	
			During the night bursts of fire on tracks between GALLWITZ and GREVILLERS LINES.	JBs
	3rd		Advance parties of AUSTRALIAN CORPS arrived.	JBs
			Bursts of fire on GALLWITZ and GREVILLERS LINES during the night & day.	JBs

WAR DIARY
or
INTELLIGENCE SUMMARY

(Erase heading not required.)

Army Form C. 2118.

Place	Date	Hour	Summary of Events and Information	Remarks and references to Appendices
BAZENTIN LE PETIT	Sept/17 4th		All batteries fired bursts of fire on GALLWITZ and GREVILLERS lines & on tracks leading to them during night & day. Observation impossible during the day owing to thick mist.	
	5th	10am	Front section of 5th Bde. 2nd Australian Div. arrived. H.Q. 5th Bde 150th	Sgs
MOLIENS au BOIS	6th to 15th		Bde in rest at MOLIENS au BOIS	Sts
OCCOCHES	16th		H.Q. B, C & D batteries marched to OCCOCHES. A battery went on to MEZEROLLES.	Sts
BOUBERS	17th		Brigade marched to BOUBERS sur CANCHE.	Sts
St. MICHEL	18th		Brigade marched to St. MICHEL. Hd.Qrs in ROELLECOURT.	Sts
	19th to 24th		Brigade in rest at St. MICHEL.	
	25th		Advance digging party of 30 men per battery proceeded to ARRAS to dig gun pits. Remainder of Bde at St MICHEL.	Sts
	26th to			

Army Form C. 2118.

WAR DIARY
or
INTELLIGENCE SUMMARY

(Erase heading not required.)

Instructions regarding War Diaries and Intelligence Summaries are contained in F. S. Regs., Part II. and the Staff Manual respectively. Title Pages will be prepared in manuscript.

Place	Date	Hour	Summary of Events and Information	Remarks and references to Appendices
ARRAS	26th to 28th		Advance party consisting of 1 officer, 32 O.R. per battery, 1 officer & 30 men from D.A.C. & 4 H.Q. signallers, prepare battery positions in ARRAS. Remainder of Bde at St. MICHEL.	

S B Davies

Major R.G.A.
Commanding 70 Bde. R.F.A.
29.2.17.

C O N F I D E N T I A L

War Diary

of

70th Bde R.F.A.

From 1st March 1917 — To 31st March 1917

Volume 91

WAR DIARY or INTELLIGENCE SUMMARY

Army Form C. 2118.

VOLUME XXI.   March 1917

Vol 19

Place	Date	Hour	Summary of Events and Information	Remarks and references to Appendices
ST. MICHEL and ARRAS	March 1917. 1st to 7th		Brigade in rest at St. Michel. Working Party – 30 men per Batty digging positions in ARRAS.	JPD
DUISANS	8th		Brigade marched to DUISANS.	JPD
"	11th		One section of C/70 came into action in it's forward position.	
ARRAS	16th	10am	70 Bde relieved 71 Bde. Batteries in action – A/70, B/70, C/70, D/70. B/71. Hd.Qrs in 22 Rue Jeanne D'arc ARRAS.	JPD
"	17th	7am	12th Div raided enemy's position. Batteries all were & carried on Barrage as ordered. The positions N.F. targets were engaged – H13 d 5.6, H14 d 4.5, H21, H26&50o5.	JPD
"	18th		Observation from unknown batter. Parties of enemy were seen a good deal during this day with good effect. Considerable movement was noticed on their front. It seems this enemy were returning & learn their front system in accordance with the general retirement.	JPD

Army Form C. 2118.

WAR DIARY
or
INTELLIGENCE SUMMARY.
(Erase heading not required.)

Instructions regarding War Diaries and Intelligence Summaries are contained in F. S. Regs. Part II. and the Staff Manual respectively. Title pages will be prepared in manuscript.

Place	Date	Hour	Summary of Events and Information	Remarks and references to Appendices
ARRAS	March/17 19th		Enemy movement was fired on with good effect in G.29.d, H.13.d, H.32.c, H.15.d & N.9.d. Hostile artillery very active.	
	20th		Much enemy movement observed fired on. Hostile artillery very active.	
	21st		"NF" targets engaged at H.27.b.99, H.27.a.95.35, H.26.d.55. Enemy aeroplanes very active an flying over new battery positions unmolested by A.A. guns or our own machines.	
	22nd & 23rd		Wire cutting overhead was carried out.	
	24th	5/pm 4. am	A large explosion observed in H.11.a. 11th Scottish Rifles raided the enemy's trenches. 15th & 12th D.A. assisted by heavies barrage fire.	
	25th	9.am 9.10 am	Party of enemy on CAMBRAI ROAD were fired at. One of our aeroplanes brought down in flames over ARRAS. 7 Smoke Balloons floated over Arras & distributed copies of the ARDENNES GAZETTE	

Army Form C. 2118.

WAR DIARY
or
INTELLIGENCE SUMMARY.
(Erase heading not required.)

Instructions regarding War Diaries and Intelligence Summaries are contained in F. S. Regs., Part II. and the Staff Manual respectively. Title pages will be prepared in manuscript.

Place	Date	Hour	Summary of Events and Information	Remarks and references to Appendices
ARRAS	March/17 25th		Wire cutting as ordered was carried out. N.F. Targets at H.34.b.59 & H.26.b.97.90. Much movement observed & fired on at H.15.c.75.	
	26th	12.30 p	Clouds of smoke were observed W of Sap W.27. Several bottles balloons up. Wire cutting as ordered.	
		3.20 pm	Number of enemy were observed in ATHIES - FAMPOUX road & fired on with good effect. Much work in Bein / carried on in HIMALAYA TRENCH.	
	27th		RAILWAY SWITCH bombarded with good effect. Smoke at H.19.b.24 was fired at.	
	28th		N.F. target at H.26.b.70.93 was engaged. Wire cutting as ordered.	
	29th		Hostile artillery very active during the day. Movement seen during the day was fired on with good effect.	
	30th		2 guns were moved into forward positions in G.22.d for wire cutting. D/70 engaged dump at H.19.d with the help of aeroplane observation.	
	31st		Wire cutting as ordered was carried out. Enemy camouflage suspected anti tank gun was engaged. Hostile artillery very active during the afternoon.	

M W Knott
Lt. Col. R.F.A.
Comdg 70 Bde R.F.A.

WAR DIARY

VOLUME XXII — 70th Bde. 15 Divn — April 1917 — Vol 20
70th Bde R.F.A.

Army Form C. 2118.

(INTELLIGENCE SUMMARY struck through)

Place	Date	Hour	Summary of Events and Information	Remarks and references to Appendices
ARRAS	1st to 2nd		Preparing to attack in front of ARRAS. Lt Col Christie commanding.	(A)
	3rd 4th		Y day: wire cutting by 18 pounders and systematic bombardment of enemy front and 2nd lines by 4.5 How & 6" Hows.	(A)
	5th		W day: wire cutting and 1st & 2nd line destruction by 16 pounders and 4.5 Hows ant batteries by the RFA and Practice Creeping barrage carried out by RGA. to BLUE LINE	(A)
	6th		X day: wire cutting & bombardment of enemy front and support lines and Heavy Artillery.	(A)
	7th		Practice Creeping barrage by 18 pounders and 4.5 Hows as far as BLUE LINE. Q day: wire cutting by 18 pounders and extensive bombardment of the enemy's defences by Heavy Artillery.	(A)
	8th		Y day: Gaps in enemy wire enlarged by 18 pounders and the enemy's Heavy Artillery engaged by H.S. Hows and Heavy Artillery. Practice Creeping Barrage carried out by 18 pounders.	(A)

ARRAS

Confidential

VOLUME XXVII

Army Form C. 2118.

WAR DIARY
INTELLIGENCE SUMMARY
(Erase heading not required.)

Instructions regarding War Diaries and Intelligence Summaries are contained in F. S. Regs., Part II. and the Staff Manual respectively. Title Pages will be prepared in manuscript.

Place	Date	Hour	Summary of Events and Information	Remarks and references to Appendices
ARRAS	9/4/17		Z day. Zero hour at 5:30 a.m. Our infantry assaulted enemy front system preceded by an artillery barrage. Our 4.5" Hows. amongst other batteries engaged counter-battery & harassing work on enemy's defences. BLACK, BLUE, BROWN and ORANGE HILL line that is German Battery positions forward of Battery positions.	A8
FEUCHY	10th		1st Division Batteries moved forward to ORANGE HILL. All Batteries in action west side of FEUCHY.	A9
	11th		10th Bde H.Q. in infantry advanced on foot. Conference at H.Q. 1st Infantry Bgde at 3 a.m. attacked at 5 a.m. MONCHY captured. Enemy brought up pack animals ammunition dump. Batteries held in the	B3
	12th		15t D.A.C. 15th D.I.V advanced and 14th Div supported 50th Div 4th Bgde attack at 6:30 p.m. unsuccessful.	B3
	13th		ROEUX NW. being captured by 9th Div on S of SCARPE S/10 had a gun hit about B/10 knock 3 men out 10th and 7th Infantry ORANGE HILL. 162nd Bgde on front of ORANGE HILL. Organizing from the reinforcements from the groups.	B3

Confidential
VOLUME XXII

WAR DIARY / INTELLIGENCE SUMMARY

Army Form C. 2118.

Place	Date	Hour	Summary of Events and Information	Remarks and references to Appendices
FEUCHY	13th inst.		C/70 moved to rear positions. Batteries shelled with gas shells all night. Placed a position. Barrage on enemy positions. 131 Central to O2 & 9.0. Batteries covered the advance of infantry from shoots on enemy communications. 162 Bde on counter-attack. Wagon lines moved to ARRAS. Communication attacked at 4 p.m. Casualties to date. Area of 1 officer and – men.	R.B.
	15th		O.R. 3 killed, 18 wounded. Division relieved. Batteries moved back to ARRAS. H.Q. wagon lines to met. at 9 a.m. 15th. Ammunition expenditure. 10858 A. 9646 AX. 3840. 45 How. 656. Each gun had 152 set at all.	R.B.
	16th		Quiet all day. FEUCHY shelled during the evening with 7.7 cm about 4.2.0.	R.B.
	17th		Helping to report all day. FEUCHY shelled slightly during the evening with 7.7 cm about 4.2.0.	R.B.
	18th		A few gun shells on Railway about H.21.d. Reconnoitered artillery positions in N.5 central. Visibility bad all day.	R.B.

Confidential
VOLUME XXII

Army Form C. 2118.

WAR DIARY
or
INTELLIGENCE SUMMARY

(Erase heading not required.)

Instructions regarding War Diaries and Intelligence Summaries are contained in F.S. Regs., Part II. and the Staff Manual respectively. Title Pages will be prepared in manuscript.

Place	Date	Hour	Summary of Events and Information	Remarks and references to Appendices
FEUCHY.	19th 4/17		Preparing for General attack. 71st Bde R.F.A. to join 70th Bde R.F.A. out from Staff Sub-Group. Communications perfected all day.	R.A.
	20th		Training and changing of various emplacements, 18 pounders and H.S. in advanced positions.	R.A.
	21st			R.A.
	22nd		Second day bombardment of all enemy positions.	R.A.
	23rd		3rd day bombardment at 4.45 am. Very heavy fighting. Our batteries advanced to support our attack all finally objectives but the first.	R.A.
	24th		71st Bde R.F.A. attacked again at 4 pm. went forward to support at new Objective.	R.A.
	25th		46th I.B. attacked and gained the objective. Our batteries heavily shelled all day. Heavy shelling of our batteries out FEUCHY throughout the day.	R.A.

2449 Wt. W14957/M90 750,000 1/16 J.B.C. & A. Forms/C.2118/12.

WAR DIARY
INTELLIGENCE SUMMARY

Army Form C. 2118.

Place	Date	Hour	Summary of Events and Information	Remarks and references to Appendices
FEUCHY	26.4.17		Batteries heavily shelled throughout the day—mostly from FEUCHY Mon. Attack at 11:30 p.m. Two counter-attacks by the enemy at night on infantry sections to the left front (KNIFE).	A.B.
	27.4.17		Quiet day. Shoe bombardment kept up all day by Bd. 18 Pdrs. on enemy's advanced trenches accompanied by Stokes.	A.B.
	28.4.17		False attack to help 12th DIV.	
	29.4.17		Subgroup repeatedly tasked by the Genl. for effective screenage — put up by 16 18 Pdrs. Diminishing all over.	A.B.
	30.4.17		Steady wants of Batty. 15 R.G.A. received & fired. Steady banter of C/170 and D/170 on enemy's communications to front positions during the night.	A.B.

MWWick Lieut-Colonel R.A.
Comdg 70th Brigade R.F.A.

CONFIDENTIAL.

WAR DIARY

of

70TH BRIGADE R.F.A.

from 1st May, 1917.   to 31st May, 1917.

(Volume 23).

WAR DIARY / INTELLIGENCE SUMMARY

Army Form C. 2118.

Place	Date	Hour	Summary of Events and Information	Remarks and references to Appendices
TILLOY	MAY 1917 1st		Moved H.Qrs of 70th Bde R.F.A. from FEUCHY to E. of TILLOY. C/70th and D/70th moved into forward positions that night. 30th – 1st. Colonel Reed on comdg 71st Bde. R.F.A. I/Gr. command of the Bde Sub Group.	A.B./1
	2nd		Preparations for the attack. A/70th and B/70th moved into forward positions during night 1st/2nd.	B.B.
	3rd		"N" day. Attacked at 3.45 am. with the 109th and 169th Bdes. Barrage ops continued to Blue Line.	B.B.
	4th		Front to within 3000 yds of Railway. All day making and improving front line.	
	5th		Ammunition dumps at the GAS WORKS. Waggon lines moved to Ors.	B.B.
	6th		Road heads to the 15th D.A.C. Quiet all day. Hostile batteries put positions.	B.B.
	7th		Quiet during the day. Own 18 pounder battalion battery to Rt. ST POL-ARRAS road on evening. A/70th Bde R.F.A. 5.90 and 4.20 battery from knocked out.	A.B./1

A/70th Bde R.F.A.

Army Form C. 2118.

WAR DIARY
or
INTELLIGENCE SUMMARY.

(Erase heading not required.)

Instructions regarding War Diaries and Intelligence Summaries are contained in F. S. Regs., Part II. and the Staff Manual respectively. Title pages will be prepared in manuscript.

Place	Date	Hour	Summary of Events and Information	Remarks and references to Appendices
TILLOY.	MAY 1917 8th		Division all day. C Ho. & Regt R.F.A. cont out of action for want of guns and men left in the position.	R.B.
	9th		Division all day.	R.B.
	10th		Division all day.	R.B.
	11th		Handing over 18 pounder ammunition to 70th Regt Artillery.	R.B.
	12th		Our infantry (168 & I.B.) attacked TOOL TR and CAVALRY FARM. TOOL TR and the first Sub Crater against from (110th & 135th Regt) only attacked at 6am.	R.B.
	13th		3rd Division attacked at 6pm. Our infantry occupied O.B. 1 & O.B. 2.	R.B.
	14th		Division commenced to be relieved. B Battery commenced relief.	R.B.
	15th		B Battery relieved. C/70 came up.	R.B.
	16th		Division all day. B/70 moved into new position. A/70 moved to handed over guns.	R.B.

WAR DIARY or INTELLIGENCE SUMMARY

Army Form C. 2118.

Place	Date Hour	Summary of Events and Information	Remarks and references to Appendices
TILLOY.	MAY 17th 1917	Quiet all day. Col. INGHAM took over the LEFT SUB GROUP. Col. CHRISTIE was C.R.A. during the General's absence.	R.S.
	18th	Col. CONOLLY commanding 70th Bde R.F.A. Quiet day. Attack at 8.20 pm. Still expected by the enemy. Their preparations for the attack.	R.S.
	19th	Quiet day. Preparations for the attack. A/10 came into the line R.B. for the attack. XVIth CORPS. Our artillery answered any enemy interference on R.B. & co. of our front.	R.B.
	20th	shelling.	R.B.
	" 21st	Quiet day. Our artillery heavily answered the enemy	R.S.
	" 22nd	Preparations for moving.	R.S.
	" 23rd	37th D.A. took over from 56th D.A.	R.S.
LAITRE-ST QUENTIN.	" 24th	The 70th and 71st Bdes R.F.A. moved to LAITRE ST QUENTIN.	R.S.
REBREUVIETTE.	" 25th	The 70th Bde R.F.A. marched to REBREUVIETTE.	R.S.
CONCHY-S-CONCHE.	" 26th	marched to CONCHY-SUR-CONCHE. Col. CHRISTIE resumed command of 70th Bde R.F.A.	R.S.

Army Form C. 2118.

WAR DIARY
or
INTELLIGENCE SUMMARY.
(Erase heading not required.)

Instructions regarding War Diaries and Intelligence Summaries are contained in F. S. Regs., Part II. and the Staff Manual respectively. Title pages will be prepared in manuscript.

Place	Date	Hour	Summary of Events and Information	Remarks and references to Appendices
CONCHY- SUR CONCHE.	27th		B.C.R.A. visited Batteries.	B.B.
	28th		General Parades & day all Batteries.	B.B.
	29th 30th 31st		MAJOR DAWBENY succeeded by 70th Bgde R.F.A. during absence of Col. CHRISTIE to U.K. General Training for all Batteries.	B.B.

CONFIDENTIAL.

WAR DIARY

of

70th BRIGADE, R. F. A.

From 1st June, 1917. To 30th June 1917.

VOLUME 24.

VOLUME № 24.

Army Form C. 2118.

WAR DIARY or INTELLIGENCE SUMMARY.

(Erase heading not required.)

Instructions regarding War Diaries and Intelligence Summaries are contained in F. S. Regs., Part II. and the Staff Manual respectively. Title pages will be prepared in manuscript.

VI 29

Place	Date	Hour	Summary of Events and Information	Remarks and references to Appendices
CONCHY-SUR-CONCHE.	JUNE 1917 1st		The 70th Brigade R.F.A. in rest at CONCHY-SUR-CONCHÉ.	R.B.
	to		On the 6th Major L. BURTON R.F.A. of D/70 was transferred to the Depôt.	R.B.
			Horse exchanging during 9th in horse field from 9th Divisional R.A.	R.B.
HEUCHIN.	16th		The 70th Brigade R.F.A. marched to HEUCHIN on the morning of the 16th.	R.B. R.B.
NORRENT FONTES.	17th		The Brigade marched to NORRENT FONTES.	R.B.
THIENNES.	18th 19th		The 70th Bgde marched to THIENNES.	R.B.
GODEWAERSVELDE.	20th		The Brigade marched to GODEWAERSVELDE.	R.B.
WATOU.	21st 22nd		The Brigade marched to the WATOU ARTILLERY AREA. and went at WATOU.	R.B.
	23rd		Preparations for going into action. Selected and battery commanders went forward to see new battery positions.	R.B.
	24th		300ft of over telephone communications from 275th Bgde R.F.A.	R.B.
			On relief of A. B. & D/70 TMB 275th Bgde R.F.A. were transferred to	
YPRES.	25th 26th 27th		Completion of relief of 275th Bgde R.F.A. by 70th Bgde R.F.A. YPRES steadily shelled all day by 5.9" and 4.2" Day Bombardment of YPRES continues.	R.B. R.B. R.B.

Army Form C. 2118.

VOLUME No XH.

WAR DIARY
or
INTELLIGENCE SUMMARY.
(Erase heading not required)

Instructions regarding War Diaries and Intelligence Summaries are contained in F. S. Regs., Part II. and the Staff Manual respectively. Title pages will be prepared in manuscript.

Place	Date Hour	Summary of Events and Information	Remarks and references to Appendices
YPRES.	1917 JUNE 28th	YPRES and the approaches heavily shelled all day. Bursts in the enemy front system in retaliation for the day's shelling of our Batty front.	R.R.
	29th	Continued bombardment of YPRES.	R.R.
	30th	Heavy shelling of the RAMPARTS and the SQARE throughout the day.	R.R.

M W A [signature] Lt Col R.F.A.
Comdg 70th Bde R.F.A.

CONFIDENTIAL.

WAR DIARY

of

70th Brigade R.F.A.

From 1st October 1917.   To 31st October, 1917.

(Volume 28).

July Aug & Sep 1917
missing

VOLUME XXVIII

Army Form C. 2118.

WAR DIARY
or
INTELLIGENCE SUMMARY.
(Erase heading not required.)

Place	Date	Hour	Summary of Events and Information	Remarks and references to Appendices
ATHIES	Oct 1917 1st		Major S.D. Graham assumed command of 70.S. Battery R.G.A.	
	2nd		Preparation of new armament commenced.	
	3rd		Calibration of 8" Howitzer guns +5" medium guns 2nd + 3rd	
	4th 5th		Commenced dismounting old position (127 & 2w)	
	5th		Continued dismounting old position & moving to reserve	
	6th		Commenced preparation of new position.	
	7th		Patients to work.	
	8th		Commenced dismounting armament in Brents in Tara & examining guns.	
	9th		Left 4 + 5th Batteries carried out shoots.	
	10th		Intermediate armament continued.	
			Wound preparations for new position.	
			Instructions on new permanent C.S.O. R.G.A.	
			Sig. Cpl P. Comments recommend commencing	
			8 70th Brigade R.G.A.	

VOLUME XXVIII

WAR DIARY
or
INTELLIGENCE SUMMARY

Army Form C. 2118.

Place	Date	Hour	Summary of Events and Information	Remarks and references to Appendices
ATHIES	Oct 11th 1917		18 pdrs engaged hostile work & D/170 carried out wire cutting.	A.A.
	12th		Gas projector bombardment on HAUSA WOOD by C coy & one section D coy. Wire cutting continued.	A.A.
	13th		18 pdrs of 191 Bde engaged hostile battery. C coy fired 6 rounds gas shell on 18th Div on left.	A.A.
	14th		4.5" Howitzers shelled COP TRENCH (I.33.b) and 18 pdrs engaged enemy working parties.	A.A.
	15th		C coy engaged enemy trenches (I.23.d.6.6). 18 pdrs destroyed A.170 in retaliation. 15/16 heavy retaliation.	A.A.
	16th		All batteries took part in artillery barrage. 18 pdrs destroyed C/170 & enemy dugouts in BIT LANE. 18 pdrs engaged PEARL TRENCH and one enemy gun.	C.C.
	17th			B.B.
	18th		18 pdr enemy trench mortar reported.	C.C.
	19th		Enemy trench mortar active near GUN TRENCH (I.27.d). 18 pdrs & Howitzers destroyed enemy defensive works.	D.D.

Army Form C. 2118.

VOLUME XXVIII

WAR DIARY
or
INTELLIGENCE SUMMARY.
(Erase heading not required.)

Instructions regarding War Diaries and Intelligence Summaries are contained in F. S. Regs., Part II. and the Staff Manual respectively. Title pages will be prepared in manuscript.

Place	Date	Hour	Summary of Events and Information	Remarks and references to Appendices
ATHIES.	Oct. 1917 20th		D/70 bombarded the western edge of DELBAR WOOD	A.S.
	21st		B/70 Supplementary bombardment carried out	A.S.
			15 Rds N.S. Incendiary	
			I 20 d — I 14 d.	
	22nd		Stationed bombardment. Preparations for Centre Heavy Artillery bombardment.	A.S.
	23rd		General bombardment carried out on experimental S.O.S. at night.	A.S.
	24th		General bombardment carried out as per programme. Raid carried out by 61st Div are supported	F.W.W.
	25th		General bombardment carried out as per programme.	F.W.W.
	26th		B/70 Bombarded POWDER TRENCH.	F.W.W.
	27th		General Bombardment carried as per programme.	F.W.W.
	28th		V/15 T.M.S Bombarded emplacement I 25 d 17.80. 18 hrs covered this bombardment.	F.W.W.

Army Form C. 2118.

VOLUME XXVIII

WAR DIARY
or
INTELLIGENCE SUMMARY.

(Erase heading not required.)

Instructions regarding War Diaries and Intelligence Summaries are contained in F. S. Regs., Part II. and the Staff Manual respectively. Title pages will be prepared in manuscript.

Place	Date Oct 1917	Hour	Summary of Events and Information	Remarks and references to Appendices
ATHIES	29th		9/10 Bombarded CARAVAN TRENCH. General Bombardment carried out as per programme.	J.W.W.
	30th		V/15 T.M.'s Bombarded × Pts. I 25 d 70.95. 18 Pdrs. covered this Bombardment.	J.W.W.
	31st		General Bombardment carried out as per programme	J.W.W.

J O Rowbotham
Lt Col
Cmdg 70 & Bde RFA

CONFIDENTIAL.

WAR DIARY

of

70th Brigade R.F.A.

(Volume 28).

From 1st November 1917. To 30th November 1917.

15th Div / Army Form C. 2118.

WAR DIARY
or
INTELLIGENCE SUMMARY.
(Erase heading not required.)

Place	Date	Hour	Summary of Events and Information	Remarks and references to Appendices
ARRAS	Nov 1917 12th		[illegible handwritten entries]	P.B.
	13th			P.B.
	14th			P.B.
	15th			P.B.
	16th			P.B.
	17th			P.B.
	18th			P.B.
	9th			P.B.
	10th			P.B.
	11th			P.B.
	12th			P.B.
	13th			P.B.
BEAUVRICOURT 14th BUS				P.B.
	15th			P.B.
	16th			P.B.
	17th			P.B.
	18th			P.B.

Army Form C. 2118.

WAR DIARY
or
INTELLIGENCE SUMMARY.
(Erase heading not required.)

Instructions regarding War Diaries and Intelligence Summaries are contained in F. S. Regs., Part II. and the Staff Manual respectively. Title pages will be prepared in manuscript.

Place	Date Nov. 1917	Hour	Summary of Events and Information	Remarks and references to Appendices
BUS.	19th		Gun sites harassment up to 6 am, then moved up after dark. Went into action — T Boy.	S.B.
HAVRINCOURT WOOD. METZ			Harassing fire in HAVRINCOURT WOOD during day from 6.30 a.m. Captured HAVRINCOURT and BIBECOURT held up in front of FLESQUIERES until 11 a.m. Advance sunk to K30 c. K30 a–c at night.	S.B.
FLESQUIERES	21st		Enemy counter-attacked FLESQUIERES and retook the village, attempt on FONTAINE. Batteries at FLESQUIERES RIDGE. H.Q. attacked and moved forward again to FLESQUIERES W. of MINE WOOD.	A.B. A.B.
	22nd		General advance and enemy reserve 3 motors. Enemy counter-attacked at night, but captured FONTAINE.	A.B.
	23rd		Attacked FONTAINE and BOURLON WOOD at 10.30 am supported by 18 pdrs & machine gun fire. 3 enemy batteries knocked out. FONTAINE will all objectives & night.	A.B.
	24th		Steady bombardment of FLESQUIERES on night's Artillery Activity. harassing fire 3 inches on S.O.S. S16.D.A.	S.B.

WAR DIARY
or
INTELLIGENCE SUMMARY.

(Erase heading not required.)

Army Form C. 2118.

Instructions regarding War Diaries and Intelligence Summaries are contained in F. S. Regs., Part II. and the Staff Manual respectively. Title pages will be prepared in manuscript.

Place	Date	Hour	Summary of Events and Information	Remarks and references to Appendices
FLESQUIÈRES	NOV 1917			
	25th		General Bombardment of FONTAINE and LA FOLIE WOOD. Considerable enemy activity. Battalion consists of 15 O.R.s. 3 Officers killed. 1 wounded, 1 O.R. killed, 20 to hospital on S.O.S. at night. Guns reached all day. Preparations for attack in FONTAINE.	A.B. A.B. A.B.
	26th		Attacked FONTAINE at 6.20 a.m. with 2nd Guards Bgde. A.R. Gained objective but driven back by enemy. Charge & and 4th V.O. killed. Guns and ammunition expended.	A.B.
	27th		Situation quieter. Batteries withdrew to wagon lines at night. Relieved by NAVRINCOURT WOOD and Renes to BUS. Unit orders to rejoin 15th Div at ARRAS.	A.B. A.B.
	28th			
	29th		Order to start by move up to position in	
	30th		@ 27. (SE of METZ). Went in to S.O.S. line. Preparations for night attack remained on S.O.S. drawn.	R.B.

30/11/17.

G B Dawkins
Lt Col R.G.A.
Cdg 70th Bgde RFA.

CONFIDENTIAL.

WAR DIARY

of

70th Brigade R.F.A.

(Volume 29).

From 1st December 1917.   to 31st December 1917.

Army Form C. 2118.

WAR DIARY
or
INTELLIGENCE SUMMARY.
(Erase heading not required.)

Instructions regarding War Diaries and Intelligence Summaries are contained in F. S. Regs., Part II. and the Staff Manual respectively. Title pages will be prepared in manuscript.

VII 28

Place	Date	Hour	Summary of Events and Information	Remarks and references to Appendices
GOUZEAUCOURT WOOD	DECEMBER 1917			
	1st		Command the GUARDS Division in the outskirts on GOUZEAUCOURT awaiting movement at [illegible]	AG
	2nd		[illegible]	AG
	3rd		GOUZEAUCOURT WOOD [illegible]	AG
	4th		[illegible]	AG
	5th		[illegible] METZ [illegible]	AG
	6th		Remained [illegible] enemy trench areas	AG
	7th		[illegible] GONNELIEU [illegible]	AG
	8th		GONNELIEU the VILLERS GUISLAIN [illegible]	BB
	9th		[illegible]	AG
	10th		[illegible] S/70 attacked and 2 [illegible] to [illegible]	[illegible]

A5834 Wt. W4973 M687 750,000 8/16 D. D. & L. Ltd. Forms/C.2118/13.

Army Form C. 2118.

WAR DIARY
or
INTELLIGENCE SUMMARY.
(Erase heading not required.)

Instructions regarding War Diaries and Intelligence Summaries are contained in F. S. Regs., Part II. and the Staff Manual respectively. Title pages will be prepared in manuscript.

Place	Date	Hour	Summary of Events and Information	Remarks and references to Appendices
COUSE AUBOURS WOOD.	DECEMBER 1917			

Army Form C. 2118.

WAR DIARY
or
INTELLIGENCE SUMMARY.
(Erase heading not required.)

Instructions regarding War Diaries and Intelligence Summaries are contained in F. S. Regs., Part II. and the Staff Manual respectively. Title pages will be prepared in manuscript.

Place	Date	Hour	Summary of Events and Information	Remarks and references to Appendices
ARRAS	DECEMBER 1917.			
	24th		[illegible handwriting]	AA.
	25th		[illegible handwriting]	
	26th		[illegible handwriting]	
	27th		[illegible handwriting]	
	28th		[illegible handwriting]	
	29th		[illegible handwriting]	AA.
	30th		[illegible handwriting]	AA.
	31st		[illegible handwriting]	
	2/2/17.		[signature] G B Dunham
Lt. Col. R.G.A.
Comm[ander] [illegible] 70th Bgd. R.G.A.	

CONFIDENTIAL.

WAR DIARY

of

70th Brigade R.F.A.

(Volume 30)

From 1st January 1918   To 31st January 1918.

Army Form C. 2118.

WAR DIARY
or
INTELLIGENCE SUMMARY.
(Erase heading not required.)

WO 29

Place	Date	Hour	Summary of Events and Information	Remarks and references to Appendices
ATHIES	JAN 1st 1918		General bombardment of enemy defensive system.	R.B.
	2nd		18 pdrs cut wire. 5" Hows firing on enemy communications & strong points.	R.B.
	3rd		Battery positions per Battery Commanders reports.	R.B.
	4th		Lieut 3/14th Bty 70th Bde RFA. Gunners D.A. Ridout sent to rest camp at HAEBACO.	R.B.
			No movement of troops.	
			Reconnaissance of new gun positions.	
			5 of 14th Bty 70th Bde RFA. 21 O.R.s & 1 Bty RFA at rest camps.	B.B.
			Remainder of Bde reconnoitred to next billets at HAEBACO.	R.B.
			No enemy activity out camp out in anno.	
HAEBACO	5th to 31st			

31/1/18.

G B Dawkins
Lt. Col. R.A.
Cdg. 70th Bde R.F.A.

CONFIDENTIAL.

WAR DIARY

of

70th Brigade R.F.A.

Volume 31.

From 1st February 1918.   To 1st March 1918.

Army Form C. 2118.

WAR DIARY
or
INTELLIGENCE SUMMARY.
(Erase heading not required.)

Instructions regarding War Diaries and Intelligence Summaries are contained in F. S. Regs., Part II. and the Staff Manual respectively. Title pages will be prepared in manuscript.

WM 30

Place	Date	Hour	Summary of Events and Information	Remarks and references to Appendices
HABARCQ	FEB. 1918.			
	1st		Battery undergoing training at HABARCQ.	A.S.
	2nd		One section sent out intermittently to ARRAS each day.	
	3rd		One section sent on detachment to Battery from R.F.A. the Running Section in the MONCHY Sector.	A.S.
	4th		Running Section of 31st Bty R.F.A. relieved by the 31st Bty	A.S.
	5th		Commanded by Capt. Sub-G Lieut. C.R. DAUBENY D.S.O. R.F.A. to 70th Bty R.F.A. Running intimation contained in 11th Corps	
MONCHY	6th		75th Bty R.F.A. GUARDS D.A. Sub. Group sent out A/70 issued instructions to Bde for carrying out night shoots 9th/10th.	A.S.
	7th			
	8th			
	9th			A.S.
	10th			
	11th			
	12th			

WAR DIARY
or
INTELLIGENCE SUMMARY

Army Form C. 2118.

Place	Date	Hour	Summary of Events and Information	Remarks and references to Appendices
MONCHY	FEB 1918			
	22nd		Preparations for Raid continued.	R.B.
	23rd		Raid Night. Registration commenced at 3.30 am. 7th Coy commenced at 11.1 am. Guns used being O.8.2, O.8.4, O.8.4, O.10.53. Registration finished by 11.50 am. Bombardment commencement difficult. Distribution of ammunition delayed by enemy shelling. 13 hours notice of raid being 4.5" How R.F.A. 6 PELVES Sector.	R.B.
	24th		Enemy artillery activity, counter battery work, and hostile shelling in PELVES Sector. Battery received ... of enemy's attempts to develop ... in hostile ...	R.B.
	25th		C/158 + A/158 A.F.A. came under Group. A/170 Batt came under ... position to position of vacated by C/170 Batt R.F.A. 6 division drawn out.	R.B.
	26th		Hostile artillery activity ... destructive ... on divisional front - Battery carried out ... and ...	R.B.

WAR DIARY
or
INTELLIGENCE SUMMARY

Army Form C. 2118.

Place	Date	Hour	Summary of Events and Information	Remarks and references to Appendices
MONCHY	FEB 1918. 27th		A/170th Bty. R.F.A. did rifle drill this morning. Aeroplanes were observed over enemy lines & our anti-aircraft guns fired on them. T.M. Pete practised firing at Refa with 1st Rifle Refa.	A.J.S.
	28th		O/170th Bty. R.F.A. went into Guards D.A. area (I.O.). Rifle drill carried out this morning. T.M. ammunition decided to fit at 12.25am	C.O.M.

G.B.Marlow
Lieut Colonel, R.G.A.
Commanding 70th Bde R.F.A.
(Sub-Group)

28/2/18.

15th Divisional Artillery.

70th BRIGADE R. F. A.

MARCH 1918

CONFIDENTIAL.

WAR DIARY

of

70th Brigade R.F.A.

(Volume 32)

From 1st March 1918.   to 31st March 1918.

Army Form C. 2118.

WAR DIARY
or
INTELLIGENCE SUMMARY.
(Erase heading not required.)

Vol. 31

Place	Date	Hour	Summary of Events and Information	Remarks and references to Appendices
Monchy	March 1918			
	1st		Retaliation fired on hostile Trench Mortars at request of Infantry & all movement engaged.	W.R.nB.
	2nd			
	3rd		Registration carried out by batteries & retaliation on hostile Trench Mortars.	W.R.nB.
	4th			
	5th		Preparation for raid & registration carried out	W.R.nB.
	6th		Raid carried out by the 10th Scottish Rifles 46th Infantry Bde at 4.40 A.M. on Enemy front line from T.3.c.3.9 to T.3.a.0.5.30. Trench was found to be empty & no prisoners were obtained — our casualties, one man wounded by M.G. fire. Hostile Trench Mortar movement engaged by Hour + 15 Rho.	W.R.nB.
	8th		Preparation for raid. Registration carried out & retaliation on Enemy Trench mortars at request of Infantry.	W.R.nB.
	9th		Raid carried out by 5th Batt. Seaforth Highlanders on enemy front line from O8.b.50.00. to O8.b.42.23. Enemy dugout line from O8.d.65.90 to O.9.a.10.35. at 5·15 A.M. which we supported with

Army Form C. 2118.

WAR DIARY
or
INTELLIGENCE SUMMARY.
(Erase heading not required.)

Place	Date	Hour	Summary of Events and Information	Remarks and references to Appendices
	March 1918. 10th		The 3rd Guards Brigade carried out a raid on Enemy trenches in I.20.a at 5pm. Two 18 Pdr Batteries & one 4.5 Hows Battery of this Brigade fired in support of this raid. During the day movement was engaged & from 9pm to 4-45pm registration was carried out on Adgil trench in I.25.d. Enemy Artillery shelled H.27.b with Gas Shells at 5-45pm (about 30 rds).	L.D.M.O
	11th		Registration was carried out during day & working parties dispersed. We retaliated on Fermoy 3 at 11-20 PM. At 6-15 pm we fired in support of Raid carried out by the 6th Battalion Cameron Highlanders on Enemy trench from O.2.d.6.2.65 to O.2.d.76.45. Enemy Artillery became active at Leuze pero 6' but as no turn was it heavy.	L.D.M.O
	12th		Working parties engaged many casualties inflicted. We also fired retaliation on hostile trench Mortars & harassing fire was carried out through the night on enemy front line as far back as Reserve trench. Enemy fired Gas Shells in H.27.b at 6-35 PM from Northind direction of Argieres.	L.D.M.O

Army Form C. 2118.

WAR DIARY
or
INTELLIGENCE SUMMARY.
(Erase heading not required.)

Instructions regarding War Diaries and Intelligence Summaries are contained in F. S. Regs., Part II. and the Staff Manual respectively. Title pages will be prepared in manuscript.

Place	Date	Hour	Summary of Events and Information	Remarks and references to Appendices
March 1918	13th		Registration carried out on Angel trench & movement engaged. Harassing fire was carried out during night	Wind ⊕
	14		Harassing fire was continued during the day on our 6" Howitzers fired on enemy wire with good results	Wind ⊕
	15		Harassing fire continued. Movement engaged in by saw toothing & working parties dispersed in Park Wood at 2.55 pm	Wind ⊕
	16		Harassing fire continued. Registration carried out & retaliation fired on hostile trench mortars as required	
	17		Infantry. All movement was engaged. Our Howitzers shelled Sevenoaks, Bucket Wood & Frosty Battery	Wind ⊕
	18		Harassing fire continued. Shrapnel being taken of sunken roads I27d & Park Wood I28d. Movement was engaged	Wind ⊕
	19		Harassing fire continued during day, movement engaged. We fired Counter Preparation South with all guns from 5.10 to 5.30 pm. Enemy retaliation in answer to our bombardment was continuous. 4.2" Gas Shell on Happy Valley, Sensée Valley, Orange Hill Battery Positions also in vicinity of Alexander	Wind ⊕
	20			

WAR DIARY
or
INTELLIGENCE SUMMARY.
(Erase heading not required.)

Place	Date	Hour	Summary of Events and Information	Remarks and references to Appendices
	March 21 1918		We fired "Bored Cambrai" from 9.10 AM to 10.40 AM. — Harassing fire No 3 was carried out afterwards & at 3pm we fired "Haraas B" with detached sections also at 7.30pm — At 9pm we commenced "Haraas 3" at increased rate of fire. — At 3 AM & 4 PM (22/3/18) we fired on "Haraas B" with all guns. During night we Gas Shelled West end of Pelves, I33c, I33c54, I33b54, Snapsot I27d, Anyclion of Right Sub. Road on "White Trench" also General Counter-preparation with Surveillance & 4.5 Hors barrage on Triston & Jacksor trenches. Enemies Artillery was fairly active all day. At 1.10pm a Smoke barrage was put down on NW of Monchy later extending to Monchy itself. Our Casualties up to date are as follows — 2 OR Killed — 10 OR wounded — Two officers wounded. Four guns damaged.	WRmR
	22		We evacuated positions in N5A & Orange Hill & occupied positions in N2d. — This retirement was carried out successfully without any casualties.	WRmR
	23		Our Artillery carried out a general bombardment on trenches in vicinity of Monchy Scarfe Valley	WRmR
	24) 25)		Harassing fire carried out & all movement engaged.	WRmR

WAR DIARY
or
INTELLIGENCE SUMMARY.
(Erase heading not required.)

Instructions regarding War Diaries and Intelligence Summaries are contained in F. S. Regs., Part II. and the Staff Manual respectively. Title pages will be prepared in manuscript.

Place	Date	Hour	Summary of Events and Information	Remarks and references to Appendices
March 1918	26		Our batteries withdrew to positions in M.6.b. continued bombarding Enemy trenches harassing fire	10h m Q 4.5 m Q
	27		All movement engaged harassing fire carried out during the night	
	28		Enemy commenced a heavy bombardment at 2-30 AM with Gas & H.E. Shells & at 4 AM he attacked on our front forcing our Infantry back to the Army line. During this attack our Artillery was heavily bombarded but fired rapidly until 10 AM when all batteries retired to Rouvillé. During this attack & movement our casualties were as follows – Killed, 2 Officers & O.R. Wounded 2 Officers 25 O.R. (1 died of wounds) Missing 2 Officers 6 O.R.	10h m Q
	29) 30) 31)		All guns were brought out safely & as such batteries proceeded to clear forward positions of Ammunition. General bombardment of enemies lines – all movement engaged harassing fire on all roads, tracks & trenches during night from Mountgun firing on selected targets such as our old H.Q. battery positions, dugouts & places likely to be accommodating the enemy.	10h m Q

G B Dankam
Lieut Colonel R.G.A.
Commanding 70th Bde R.G.A.

15th Divisional Artillery

70th BRIGADE R. F. A.

APRIL 1 9 1 8

CONFIDENTIAL.

WAR DIARY

of

70th Brigade R.F.A.

(Volume 33).

From 1st April 1918.   To 30th April 1918.

Army Form C. 2118.

WAR DIARY
or
INTELLIGENCE SUMMARY.
(Erase heading not required.)

Instructions regarding War Diaries and Intelligence Summaries are contained in F. S. Regs., Part II. and the Staff Manual respectively. Title pages will be prepared in manuscript.

W.6.3.7

Place	Date	Hour	Summary of Events and Information	Remarks and references to Appendices
April 1918	13th 10th & 11th		All movement working parties engaged & dispersed by our Artillery. Shoots were carried out on dugouts, Gun Pits, our Barrage Fire with successful reaults - Harassing fire was carried on during night on Roads, Tracks, Beaumetz & Centres of movement. Enemy Artillery on the whole was Quiet but our front support lines were heavily shelled at times with 4.2s, 5.9s & shrapnel from the direction of Monchy	R.B.
	12th 10th 13th		Harassing fire carried out in accordance with DA Programme. All movement was engaged, working parties dispersed. Enemy Artillery was rather active at times on Tilloy, Battery Valley, Narrow Ridge & Battery positions Arras East was intermittently shelled by H.V. Guns.	R.B.
	14th 15th 16th		Harassing fire carried out as ordered. Considerable movement was observed during this period, especially on Cromarty, Invergordon & California Trenches. This was engaged by our Artillery. Enemy Artillery was quiet except for a few bursts of shrapnel in vicinity of "Aldero" O.P. A few A.A. shell fell in Arras.	R.B.
	14th		Harassing fire as ordered. Movement Engaged, dispersed in No 1 - Machine Gun emplacement in Sap at M.33.C.14. was knocked out by one of our batteries during the afternoon. - Enemy Arty quiet.	R.B.

WAR DIARY
or
INTELLIGENCE SUMMARY.
(Erase heading not required.)

Army Form C. 2118.

Instructions regarding War Diaries and Intelligence Summaries are contained in F. S. Regs., Part II. and the Staff Manual respectively. Title pages will be prepared in manuscript.

Place	Date	Hour	Summary of Events and Information	Remarks and references to Appendices
April 1916	18th 19th 20th		Harassing fire continued during nights — all movement observed was engaged — dispersed by our Artillery — At 6.30 AM on the 20th we fired in support of our Infantry attack on Enemy trenches in K.37.c. This attack was very successful. The posts were captured & held — thirty two prisoners & some machine guns were taken — Our casualties were very slight.	R.B.
	21, 22 23rd 24th 25th		Harassing fire carried out as ordered & movement engaged. The enemy put down a heavy barrage on our front subsequent to the evening of the 24th following a raid carried out by the Brigade on our right — We retaliated & searched 500 yds from our S.O.S.	R.B.
	26th 27th 28th 29th 30th		Guns silent — On the evening of the 29th the Brigade came out of action & proceeded to Wagon Lines at Fauquière. Brigade marched to Reg.	R.B.

E B Davies
Lieut. Col.
Com'dg. 1/4th 3rd Bde R.F.A.

C O N F I D E N T I A L.

WAR DIARY

of

70th Brigade R.F.A.

(Volume 17.)
[34]

From 1st May 1918.

To 31st May 1918.

Army Form C. 2118.

WAR DIARY
or
INTELLIGENCE SUMMARY.
(Erase heading not required.)

Instructions regarding War Diaries and Intelligence Summaries are contained in F. S. Regs., Part II. and the Staff Manual respectively. Title pages will be prepared in manuscript.

Place	Date 1918	Hour	Summary of Events and Information	Remarks and references to Appendices
	Mar. 1st 2nd 3rd 4th		Marched from Danville 16 Aug where Brigade remained at rest until the night of the 3rd At 9 PM on the morning of the 4th this Brigade took over the front covered by the 4th C.F.U. occupying positions in A 1, 8, 24, 30 & B 13, 19 east of Rocluncourt	JR JR
	5th 10th 11th		Registrations carried out & our Forward Sections engaged enemy movement & fired on special targets at request of infantry.	JR
	12th to 25th		Harassing fire was carried out each night on tracks, railways, roads & avenues of movement — Movement during the daytime was engaged & many casualties inflicted — 18th Bn Batteries alternately moved one gun forward by Decauville at night to the vicinity of Bailleul & harassed enemy tracks & roads to extreme range — Our Hows carried out several successful shoots with Aeroplane observation. During the month our main positions, apart from Registrations, have remained silent — One Gun from each 18 Pdr Forward Section was withdrawn to main positions & One How from main positions was moved forward to Detached Section.	JR
	26th		Harassing fire was carried out during night — Little movement was observed during day	JR
	27th		Harassing fire was carried out & enemy infantry on roads and tracks. At 2.0 AM battery positions were heavily shelled with gas.	JR
	28th		Harassing fire was carried out and movement observed was fired on. Howitzers fired on targets in C 25 a & b, C 19 d, C 20 c and C 19 b	JR

Army Form C. 2118.

WAR DIARY
or
INTELLIGENCE SUMMARY.
(Erase heading not required.)

Place: ROCLINCOURT

Date	Hour	Summary of Events and Information	Remarks and references to Appendices
May 1918 29-	2 pm	Coy H.Q. in B.29.a.0.8.4 was fired on. Movement observed in B.20.6.8.9 was fired on. During the night harassing fire was carried out on BELVOIR ALLEY, Railway in C.19.d, HOLLOW COPSE, SQUARE WOOD and COUNT TRENCH. Howitzers searched C.O.D and CRAWL trenches and roads in C.25.a and 6. C.19.a & 6 C.20.a and C.25.c.	JSS
	6.45 pm		
30th		During the night harassing fire was carried out on - BRADFORD, BELVOIR, CHESTNUT and CROP TRENCHES. Roads in C.20.a & 6, C.19.c & d, C.20.c, C.21.c, C.25.a & c. 12 pdrs. Hows fired on GAVRELLE- FRESNES Road, C.O.D and CRAWL Trenches and Bastion C.20.a & 6 a C.25.c. Some hostile balloons up. Much aerial activity.	JSS
31st		Harassing fire was carried out during the night by 18 pdrs on - Trenches, roads and railways in the Brigade zone. D/70 took a H.O. forward to H.2.c.9.7 and fired on roads, tracks and decauvilles and a dump at C.27.c.65.35. Enemy aircraft very active.	JSS

1.6.18.

G.O. Darley

Lieut. Col. R.G.A.
Comdg. 7th BdeR.F.A.

CONFIDENTIAL.

WAR DIARY

OF

70th Brigade R.F.A.

(volume 35)

From 1st June 1918. To 30th June 1918.

WAR DIARY or INTELLIGENCE SUMMARY.

70th Bde R.F.A.

Vol 34

Place	Date	Hour	Summary of Events and Information	Remarks and references to Appendices
ROCLINCOURT	June 1918 1st		Forward guns (18pdrs) carried out harassing fire during the night on tracks used by the enemy. Howrs carried out harassing fire on road junctions, light railways and communication trenches.	J81
	2nd		During the day a 77 mm gun reported active by 18pdrs, several direct hits been obtained. Several parties of the enemy were dispersed. During the night in addition to the usual harassing fire, Hows. carried out a lethal shell bombardment on enemy dugouts, 18pdrs searching the area with Shrapnell.	J82
	3rd 5th 6th 7th		During the day all movement seen was engaged. A night wire harassing fire on enemy forward communication. Hows fired on an enemy wire with good effect. 18pdrs fired on a dump in C.21. Usual harassing fire.	J83 J84

Army Form C. 2118.

WAR DIARY
or
INTELLIGENCE SUMMARY.

70ᵗʰ Bde R.F.A.

(Erase heading not required.)

Instructions regarding War Diaries and Intelligence Summaries are contained in F. S. Regs., Part II. and the Staff Manual respectively. Title pages will be prepared in manuscript.

Place	Date	Hour	Summary of Events and Information	Remarks and references to Appendices
	June 1918.			
ROCLINCOURT	8ᵗʰ		During the day Hows fired on enemy posts and front system - Normal Harassing fire.	App
	9ᵗʰ		All guns and Hows fired in support of the gas Beam attack. Normal Harassing fire.	App
	10ᵗʰ 11ᵗʰ		Normal Harassing fire and Sniping (by Harassing Guns.	App
	12ᵗʰ		15-pdr Anti-Tank gun fired a test of 30 rounds. Normal Harassing fire.	App
	13ᵗʰ to 17ᵗʰ		Normal night harassing fire and Sniping (by Harassing Guns.	App
	18ᵗʰ		15ᵗʰ Divl Arty relieved by 51ˢᵗ Divl Arty. Brigade remained at wagon lines at ÉCURIE.	App
BLANGY ÉCURIE	19ᵗʰ to 21ˢᵗ		Brigade at wagon lines at ÉCURIE	App
	22ⁿᵈ		15ᵗʰ Divl Arty relieved 2ⁿᵈ Divl Artyᵉᵛᵉⁿⁱⁿᵍ 15ᵗʰ Divl front. 70ᵗʰ Bde relieved A/1ˢᵗ Bde R.F.A. at BLANGY CHATEAU	App

Army Form C. 2118.

WAR DIARY
or
INTELLIGENCE SUMMARY.

70th Bde R+A.

(Erase heading not required.)

Instructions regarding War Diaries and Intelligence Summaries are contained in F. S. Regs. Part II. and the Staff Manual respectively. Title pages will be prepared in manuscript.

Place	Date	Hour	Summary of Events and Information	Remarks and references to Appendices
BLANGY CHATEAU	June 23rd 1918		Registration of new Zones carried out. Normal Harassing fire.	ffs
	24th		7/8th KOSB: carried out a raid on ICELAND TRENCH. 2. 18 pdr Batteries barraged ICELAND TRENCH 1. 18 pdr Battery bombarded old gun pits in "no mans land" just south of pill Zone raided Howitzers bombarded Trench mortars. Normal Harrassing fire.	ffs ffs
	25th			
ARRAS	26th		Bde H.Q. moved to No 6 Place St Croix, ARRAS. Normal Harrassing fire.	ffs
	27th		Normal Harrassing fire. N.F calls received was answered by Howitzers.	ffs
	28th		Enemy aircraft very active. During the night a letter shell bombardment was carried out by Hows in conjunction with the Heavies. 18 pdrs harrassed the Zone & in the rear of the ridge — WELFORD TRENCH. Aircraft very active.	ffs

Army Form C. 2118.

WAR DIARY
or
INTELLIGENCE SUMMARY.
(Erase heading not required.)

Instructions regarding War Diaries and Intelligence Summaries are contained in F.S. Regs., Part II. and the Staff Manual respectively. Title pages will be prepared in manuscript.

Place	Date	Hour	Summary of Events and Information	Remarks and references to Appendices
ARRAS	June 1918 29th		Normal Harassing fire. Retaliation on enemy m.r. system, T.M.'s and Batteries were carried out at the request of the infantry.	183
	30		Normal Harassing fire was carried out. Portion of H30c 4.8 was kept under fire during the day at request of H.A.G. Have registered battle Batteries HD P1 by aeroplane observation. Three enemy balloons up.	183

30.6.18.

J Starling Lieut R.T.A.
for Lieut. Col. R.G.A.
Commanding 70th Bde R.F.A.

CONFIDENTIAL.

WAR DIARY

of

70th Brigade R.F.A.

(Volume 36.)

From 1st July 1918 to 31st July 1918.

Army Form C. 2118.

70th Bde R.F.A. WAR DIARY or INTELLIGENCE SUMMARY.

VII 36

(Erase heading not required.)

Instructions regarding War Diaries and Intelligence Summaries are contained in F. S. Regs., Part II. and the Staff Manual respectively. Title pages will be prepared in manuscript.

Place	Date	Hour	Summary of Events and Information	Remarks and references to Appendices
ARRAS	July 1918 1st to 7th		During the day Support and Counter Battery work carried out by forward guns and Howitzers. During the night Harassin' fire executed on Railways, roads, Tracks, bridges etc.	$PA
	8th	9.50 pm	The division on our right carried out a raid on some old quarries in "no mans land" capturing 4 prisoners and killing many of the enemy. Our forward guns and howitzers put a Smoke Barrage on ICELAND TRENCH which appeared very successful.	$PA
	9th to 13th		A/70 moved their main position to the 1st Siegfried position Wgt2 R Schrs. Homer Harrowin' and Counter Battery work and Support.	$P3
	14th		Sections relieved by 1st Bde C.F.A.	$P3
ACQ	15th		Bde relieved by 1st Bde C.F.A. March to ACQ.	$P3
	16th	10 pm	Bde marched to TINCQUES C/70 to SAVY.	$P4
	17th	8.30 am	Entrained at TINCQUES - St POL - DOULLENS, AMIENS, POIX, BEAUVAIS, NOGENT, CLERMONT. detrained at CLERMONT 11 pm.	$P5
	18th	4 am	Marched to NOINTEL	$P5
	19th		March to Pont de la Croix - note Pont St MAXENCE and VERBERIE.	$P5
VIEUX MOULIN	20th	8 am	Bde marched to VIEUX MOULIN via St JEANNE au BOIS.	$P5

A5834 Wt. W4973 M687 750,000 8/16 D D. & L. Ltd. Forms/C.2118/13.

Army Form C. 2118.

WAR DIARY
or
INTELLIGENCE SUMMARY.
(Erase heading not required.)

Place	Date	Hour	Summary of Events and Information	Remarks and references to Appendices
MORTE FONTAINE	July 1918 21st	6 am	Bde marched to MORTE FONTAINE via RETEUIL	JB3
ST PIERRE AIGLE	22nd		15th Div marched to ST PIERRE AIGLE area. And 1 Sect Hv Batty go into action with 1st U.S.G. division.	JB4
CHAUDIN	23rd		Bde relieved Regt 1st U.S. div. near CHAUDIN.	JB5
	28th	12.50 pm	15th Div 44th Bde attacked and took BUZANCY. 70th Bde fired creeping and protective barrages. Division on right were not successful. 11th Div had to retire to original line. 250 prisoners including 30 officers taken.	JB8
	29th-30th		15th Div Infantry took over front of Div on right. 70th & 71st Btries remain in action. 87th FRENCH division.	JB9
	31st		Enemy artillery activity increasing from the North. Gas shells been used for Hannonin[?] roads and valleys.	JB

Field.
31.7.18.

G. B. Dewhurst[?]
Lieut. Col. R.G.A.
Comdg 70th Bde R.G.A.

CONFIDENTIAL.

WAR DIARY

of

70th Brigade R. F. A.

From 1st August 1918.   To 31st August 1918.

(Volume 37).

WAR DIARY or INTELLIGENCE SUMMARY

Army Form C. 2118.

(Erase heading not required.)

Instructions regarding War Diaries and Intelligence Summaries are contained in F. S. Regs., Part II. and the Staff Manual respectively. Title pages will be prepared in manuscript.

Place	Date AUGUST 1918.	Hour	Summary of Events and Information	Remarks and references to Appendices
CHAUDUN	1st		Situation E. of CHAUDUN. Reported the enemy in BUZANCY village. Patrols sent to reconnoitre BUZANCY - CHARTREUVE - VILLEMONTOIRE.	R.S.
	2nd		Enemy withdrawing during the night. Our patrols sent forward.	R.S.
			Outposts N.E. and N. of BUZANCY village. Movement of enemy. 45th Bat (?) took 15 prisoners	
			E. of BUZANCY village. At 9.0 p.m. right Battn. of 3rd Bde. reached edge of wood - Bois de Courjumelles.	
DOMMIERS	3rd		Reconnaissance of the Wagon lines.	R.S.
RALLY	4th		Marched at 6 am to RALLY, arrived at 8.30 am. about 50 kilometres.	R.S.
LIGNEVILLE	5th		LIGNEVILLE on the PONT-St-MAXENCE front.	R.S.
ETREE-WAMIN	6th		Detrained at FREVENT during the afternoon. Marched at 12.30 am to ETREE-WAMIN.	
	6th		Arrived at ETREE-WAMIN.	
	17th		On the SOISSONS FRONT.	R.S.
PGNY	17th		Inspection of the 160th Battn. here and also went on Parade H.Q. Section practised. Reconnaissance of the training area during the morning.	R.S.
	31st		Continued carrying out training.	R.S.

Army Form C. 2118.

WAR DIARY
or
INTELLIGENCE SUMMARY.
(Erase heading not required.)

Instructions regarding War Diaries and Intelligence
Summaries are contained in F. S. Regs., Part II.
and the Staff Manual respectively. Title pages
will be prepared in manuscript.

Place	Date	Hour	Summary of Events and Information	Remarks and references to Appendices
	AUGUST 1918.			
AGNY	18th to 25th		In action at AGNY. Bonnert Wagon Lines moved forward to AGNY CHATEAU to admire to admiss battery positions.	R.B.
TILLOY	26th		Batteries moved forward during night Aug 25/26 to new positions. Battn. H.Qr. moved to pumping station E of AGNY. Company Bonnert sent at 3 am in support of attack by 2nd Canadian Division. B. attacker & new 1st & E of BOIS-des-BŒUFS. Batteries went into action day of onw.	R.B.
NEB (Map S16 NW)	27th		10 positions NW of WAHCOURT. Cue MAPPE attacked unsuccessfully by 4th Div. E of WANCOURT. Batteries out of action.	R.B.
WANCOURT	29th		Outlook VIS-EN-ARTOIS field taken by OCEAN WORK. Wancourt Comment of 1/70 Bde R.F.A. GRAHAM. M.C. & 1/70 Bde R.F.A. SAWREY D.S.O. attack by Brit.	R.B.
	30th		outlook UPTON wounded. Major S.J. Dinnmoore in charge.	R.B.
	31st		Captured communication by 1st Canadian Division.	R.B.
			OCEAN WORK captured.	R.B.

M.G. Robinson
Lieut Col. R.F.A.
Cmdg. 70 Bde R.F.A.

9/9/16.

CONFIDENTIAL.

WAR DIARY

of

70th Brigade R.F.A.

(volume. 38)

From 1st September 1918.   To 30th September 1918.

Army Form C. 2118.

WAR DIARY
or
INTELLIGENCE SUMMARY.
(Erase heading not required.)

Vol 37

Place	Date	Hour	Summary of Events and Information	Remarks and references to Appendices
ST POLAY AUTHORNE Valley of the SENSEE	Sept. 1		Canadian attacked, captured PUNY. Cavalry advance on front on canal du NORD - went to menlk position S.E. of BOIRY	AN
BOIRY S.E.	2		Covering 11th Division of Infantry	AN
	3		Enemy and Railway gone on wagon lines - heavy bombing raids	AN
	4		However carry out R.G. quand the left flank.	AN
	5		Released by 58th D.A. - moved back to ARRAS for the night	AN
ARRAS	6		marched to HERSIN	AN
HERSIN	7		On section for battery link over from 55th Bde, 11th D.A., in the LOOS SECTOR (Right Sector I Corps)	AN
	8		Relief completed, covering 46th (N) Bde, 51st Division	AN
	9		Came out Regulthelt & Harasing fire made preparation for a relief with 24th Divisional rifle	AN
	10		24th Div. relieved at 5:30 a.m. No identification several casualties nil.	MW
	11			
	12		General preparation for advance, position advanced for forward portion ammunition	MW
	13		B/118 was own attached to R/115 Regt vah 150B	MW
	14		Took over 2 coy but from Division a left forward cash available R/left Bde attack St ELIE	MW
	15		further preparation was made for Raid	MW
	16			
	17		2.50 POTTER A. PIELO - ASPINALL were killed near POSTS 7 & AUTHONE. OG/BdE raids HULLUCH Trench - found normal	MW
	18		Casualties nil. Lieuts Knowles fer Foreman taken. D/70 On line worthe rel. to BRACQUEMONT	AW

(A8604)   D. D. & L., London, E.C.   Wt. W1771/M231 750,000   5/17   Sch. 52   Forms/C218/14

Army Form C. 2118.

WAR DIARY
or
INTELLIGENCE SUMMARY.
(Erase heading not required.)

Instructions regarding War Diaries and Intelligence Summaries are contained in F. S. Regs., Part II. and the Staff Manual respectively. Title pages will be prepared in manuscript.

Place	Date	Hour	Summary of Events and Information	Remarks and references to Appendices
	19		} Nothing seen for fourteen	M4
	20			H4
	21			K4
	22		Preparation were made for projector attack.	K4
	23		Wagon lines of B/70 & B/70 moved to BAPLIN Projector attack by left Bde	M4 R4
				S4
	28		} Carried out wearing tests by gas { forward gun emp together wire cutting
	29		} and tests on the enemy trenches to day. {
	30		} { Raid by Rt Bde. No prisoners, 7 casualties.
			10 am

T.G. Robinson
Lieut Colonel RFA
Commanding 70th Bde. RFA.

1/10/16.

CONFIDENTIAL

War Diary

of

70th Bde R.F.A.
15' Divn

From 1/10/18 to 31/10/18

Volume 39.

Army Form C. 2118.

WAR DIARY
INTELLIGENCE SUMMARY.
(Erase heading not required.)

Instructions regarding War Diaries and Intelligence Summaries are contained in F. S. Regs., Part II. and the Staff Manual respectively. Title pages will be prepared in manuscript.

Place	Date	Hour	Summary of Events and Information	Remarks and references to Appendices
LOOS. ELMASTON CASTLE	October 1st		A day of quiet. Simas preparation were made for an enemy withdrawal	App.
	2nd		Left Bde took a prisoner, who stated that the enemy were withdrawing at 4. a.m. that day. This statement was correct, and by the end of the day, our infantry had advanced with little opposition to the CITÉ-ST-LAURENT — HULLUCH — LA BASSÉE line. The VENDIN-DOUVRIN line was held by the enemy.	ASW.
	3rd		During the night Batteries moved up to positions in G 36 and H 31. Headquarters did not move. The enemy evacuated the VENDIN-DOUVRIN line at 9 a.m., and it was occupied by our troops at about the same time. Nine prisoners were captured by Right Bde in the morning. By the evening our troops had reached a line which included the WEST of VENDIN, and just WEST of METALLURGIQUE works. At the end of the day patrols were pushing forward of this line, keeping VENDIN-DOUVRIN line as main line of Resistance. During the day an advance H.Q. was kept open in our old front line in H 32 a. (A4a N.W 1/20,000). At night A/70 — B/70 — B/155 — 2 gun D/70 moved forward.	App.
	4th		The day was fairly quiet, and the line remained substantially the same. In the evening the Right Bde attacked to capture VENDIN and establish a line on West bank of CANAL DE LA HAUTE DEULE. They took 2 prisoners but met heavy M.G. fire, which caused them to a line. Nevertheless, during the night, patrols pushed forward and the COKE OVENS and the church were occupied. At night B/155 and 4 gun D/70 moved forward.	App.
	5th		The day passed so tranquilly. Busily, the enemy artillery being exceptionally quiet. Left Bde crowded in the evening, but did not reveal anything.	App.

Army Form C. 2118.

WAR DIARY
or
INTELLIGENCE SUMMARY.
(Erase heading not required.)

Instructions regarding War Diaries and Intelligence Summaries are contained in F. S. Regs., Part II. and the Staff Manual respectively. Title pages will be prepared in manuscript.

Place	Date	Hour	Summary of Events and Information	Remarks and references to Appendices
LOOS ELVASTON CASTLE	October 6		In the morning the enemy attacked our post in VENDIN, attacking with a company along the North and a company along the South. Our posts with drew, and after a sharp bombardment, they reoccupied their old line. Subsequent to this Heavy and field Artillery bombarded the part of the village which we do not hold. Enemy Artillery was generally quiet, and own especially active.	AAA
	7		Our patrols again tried to push out, and again met with opposition. Accordingly the 6" Hows and 18 pdrs bombarded the enemy posts. Generally, the day was very quiet, with little Hostile Artillery activity	AAA
	8		Infantry action NIL. Heavy and Field Artillery carried out several bombardments of the East of VENDIN and the Coke ovens. Hostile Artillery was markedly more active	AAA
	9		Preparation was commenced for an attack to capture the whole of VENDIN and establish our line on the canal. Infantry action nil and Enemy artillery normal.	AAA
	10		The preparatory bombardment for the attack was commenced.	AAA
	11		The attack was cancelled. Active Harassing fire was carried out by day and night	AAA
	12		It was decided to attack VENDIN. After some two hours bombardment, the attack was launched at 15.30. All objectives were captured, our line being established Roo yards West of CANAL DE LA HAUTE DEULE. 30 prisoners were captured. As to a further withdrawal was very scanty and contradictory.	AAA

Army Form C. 2118.

WAR DIARY
or
~~INTELLIGENCE SUMMARY~~
(Erase heading not required.)

Instructions regarding War Diaries and Intelligence Summaries are contained in F. S. Regs., Part II. and the Staff Manual respectively. Title pages will be prepared in manuscript.

Place	Date	Hour	Summary of Events and Information	Remarks and references to Appendices
ELVASTON CASTLE	Oct 1918 13		Our patrols were pushed forward N. of VENDIN and the enemy was found not to occupy the WEST bank of the canal. We took over more line to the right, thus including ANNAY in the Bn Zone.	ASct
"	14		Patrols pushed forward on Rt Bn Front. They could not reach Hovasin I27a (4&Nw) owing to M.G. fire	ASct
"	15		Hovasin in I27a was raided and found unoccupied – our patrols crossed canal on the whole front, and by 0900 am Bns reached a general line through I20 central. No opposition was met and a section of Howitzers and 18pdn moved up to position just west of the canal at 10.00. In the evening A17a & B17a crossed the canal, and coming into position in I13b and I26 respectively. Infantry established themselves on the general line FOSSE 6 de MEURCHIN (inclusive) – ESTEVELLES inclusive. HQ moved to VENDIN, opening there at 5 pm	ASct
VENDIN	16		The infantry pushed on at dawn and passed through CARVIN during the day. By dusk the battalion had occupied position about FOSSE 4 de CARVIN. HQ opened at Quarry at 10 a.m. At 20.00 the infantry were established in a general line H.N. & S. through I 31 with patrols believed through BOIS D'EPINOY. The enemy shelled CARVIN they last the day	ASct
QUARRY I20c.0.50.				

Army Form C. 2118.

WAR DIARY
or
INTELLIGENCE SUMMARY.
(Erase heading not required.)

Instructions regarding War Diaries and Intelligence Summaries are contained in F. S. Regs., Part II. and the Staff Manual respectively. Title pages will be prepared in manuscript.

Place	Date	Hour	Summary of Events and Information	Remarks and references to Appendices
Quarry Troc (L6a) and LIBERCOURT	Oct 1918 17		The infantry pushed on at dawn, meeting with no opposition. By nightfall they had reached a general line through N10 S.5 through K10 and K.6. Except situation of front troops was slightly uncertain. During the afternoon Batteries moved up to position of rear divns about LIBERCOURT. Headquarters were established at LIBERCOURT at 16.30 hrs.	A App
LIBERCOURT and DRUMEZ	18		The infantry again pushed forwards. At 14.30 hrs they were established on a general line through K27 and K25. There was more M.G. fire than heretofore. In the early morning position of rear divns of the Batteries were reconnoitred and occupied about DRUMEZ in K9d. H Q established there at 10 a.m. Enemy Artillery was slightly more active towards the evening, although there appeared to be two or perhaps three batteries in action. One of these was a 15cm Hun Btys Rgm. This was the first time a heavy battery has been noticed in action since the commencement of the enemy's retirement.	App
GENECH CHATEAU PBURAU LAVERDERE	19		The infantry carried on their advance, and by nightfall were established on a general line North and South line through L.6 & 17. Batteries occupied positions in rear divns around MOLPAS (44.L2a) and LAVERDERIE (44.L.1d)	App
LAVERDERIE, GENECH CHATEAU and PBURCY	20		461.1B took over He lur and 70 H Bde became advanced fund Artillery. 19/70 was attached to Outpost battalion and did useful work against enemy M.G.c. The remainder occupied position in readiness around PBURCY in the stages. The came on, and objective was gained.	App

WAR DIARY
or
INTELLIGENCE SUMMARY

(Erase heading not required.)

Army Form C. 2118.

Place	Date	Hour	Summary of Events and Information	Remarks and references to Appendices
BERCU - PETIT RUMES (44 S.7.a.)	21/10/18		By nightfall the infantry were established on a general line 400 yards west of the canal. At night the enemy artillery was fairly active and led to the opinion that the enemy would make a stand R. of the canal, accordingly a counter battery organization was formed consisting of C/70 and 160pdr. Two O.P's at opposite flanks of Divisional front were established, and flares were utilised. This organisation was under the command of Major S.D. GRAHAM M.C., O.C. C/70. A/70 was again under the orders of the Outpost battalion commander. The situation in the morning was not very clear. The enemy carried out a low flying reconnaissance about 0900. Then was the first enemy aeroplane seen since the commencement of the retirement from the HAUTE DEULE CANAL. Hostile artillery was markedly active. In the evening an enemy patrol, set for li lui hours in HOLLAIN (44.D.5.) and attacked one of our patrols. There men were driven off by LEWIS GUN and rifle fire.	Kar.
PETIT RUMES	22/10/18			Kar.
PETIT RUMES	22/10/18		Enemy Artillery was still very active. Infantry situation was unchanged. One Section of 6" Hows. (45B) and Section 1/1 LANCS HTB 60pdr battery, were in action by 16th day for Counter Battery purposes. X. V. gun were active on back areas by night with harassing fire on roads, approaches etc.	

Army Form C. 2118.

WAR DIARY
or
INTELLIGENCE SUMMARY.
(Erase heading not required.)

Instructions regarding War Diaries and Intelligence Summaries are contained in F. S. Regs., Part II. and the Staff Manual respectively. Title pages will be prepared in manuscript.

Place	Date	Hour	Summary of Events and Information	Remarks and references to Appendices
PETIT RUMES	24/10/18		Infantry situation unchanged - Enemy Artillery very active during night, less so by day. HQ moved to the LAITERIE B6c 0.0. (44).	Appx.
PETIT RUMES	25/10/18		Infantry situation unchanged. Enemy Artillery was quiet by day, but extremely active by night. During the night the Division on the right (58th) consolidated & dug in on the Canal. The enemy Rearing evacuated MAULDE (44. I.) and FLENARIES (44. Q.25.)	Appx.
PETIT RUMES	26/10/18		Our officer patrol crossed the canal by the Railway Bridge at V.21.c.9.5. & proceeded 500 yds into Howarth undercountered no enemy. Flashing guns were encountered from the North. HQ moved to 44 C.i.c. central at 1300hrs. Enemy harassing fire during the night was slightly below normal.	Appx.
PETIT RUMES	27/10/18		C day of quiet. Enemy Artillery was very quiet. One enemy T.M. was in action shelling BRUYELLE (37.V.26). Several civilians were arrested as being enemy agents. These were evacuated under escort and the result of their examination was not heard. The weather, which had been fine for some days, broke and there were several heavy showers. Major Graham M.C. R.F.A. (C/70 Bde) Coord ki fence fic. as Counter Battery officer, on the Corps Counter Battery office camerile line, with HQ division at LA GLANERIE (44 B.16.b). At date the 70th Bde.RFA was distributed as follows A) 70 - 6 guns in action at 44.C.4.a.45.50 . B) 70 - 2 guns " " 37.O.30.a.20.50 C) 70 - 4 guns " in rednwment 44 C.9.a.30.50. D) 70 - 6 guns " " in readment of 44 C.9.c.43.60. D/70 - 6 Hows in action at 44 C.12.c.10.60.	Appx. 1/1 Lancs H.B. 6o pdrs 2 guns C9c 20.20 (44) 4 S.B. 6" Hows 2 Hows 44 C.12a 20. 60.

Army Form C. 2118.

WAR DIARY
or
INTELLIGENCE SUMMARY.
(Erase heading not required.)

Instructions regarding War Diaries and Intelligence Summaries are contained in F. S. Regs., Part II. and the Staff Manual respectively. Title pages will be prepared in manuscript.

Place	Date	Hour	Summary of Events and Information	Remarks and references to Appendices
PETIT RUMES	27/10/18		(Continued) Should the Division on the left reach the canal the 15th Division was to relieve Nath, for the purpose of crossing the canal. Should this fare to be done by force, the infantry would attack under a barrage. The following barrows were accordingly reconnoitred. A/70 37U30d 9.5.20 B/70 37 V 25 c 10.30. C/70 U 30 a 20 5 0 (present section position) D/70 44 C 12 c 10.60 (present position)	A/see
"	28/10/18		The day was only marked by the burst of the Hostile Artillery by day – At night the enemy harassing fire was not so heavy.	A/see
"	29/10/18		Another quiet day – An enemy aeroplane was shot down in the morning. Enemy Artillery was again active by night. Others were of the opinion that the most part of the enemy guns came up by night for harassing purposes, being withdrawn in the morning. This theory was borne out by the fact that the heaviest harassing fire began some hours after dark, and ended some hours before dawn.	A/see
"	30/10/18		The most noticeable feature of the day was the Propaganda enemy airplane activity. Some of these planes dropped Peace propaganda pamphlets, harping on a somewhat new theme, namely that the Pan German do not influence or control German sentiment, but that some laborer in the Central Powers want the Entente Powers was of a like nature, and striving for like ideals, what barrier was is there to Peace?	A/see

D. D. & L., London, E.C. (A8024) Wt. W1771/M2531 750,000 5/17 Sch. 52 Forms/C2118/14

Army Form C. 2118.

WAR DIARY
or
INTELLIGENCE SUMMARY.
(Erase heading not required.)

Place	Date	Hour	Summary of Events and Information	Remarks and references to Appendices
PETIT RUMES	31/10/18		The day was very quiet. Hostile Harassing fire by night was also much less. The 46th I.B., having been relieved the night 29/30, the 70th Bde R.F.A. came under the orders of the 44 I.B., General Thompson commanding.	

M Robinson
Lieut Colonel R.F.A
Commanding 70th Bde RFA

CONFIDENTIAL.

WAR DIARY.

of

70th Brigade R.F.A.

(Volume 40).

From 1st November 1918. **To 30th November 1918.**

WAR DIARY or INTELLIGENCE SUMMARY

Army Form C. 2118.

NOVEMBER 1918

(Erase heading not required.)

Instructions regarding War Diaries and Intelligence Summaries are contained in F. S. Regs., Part II. and the Staff Manual respectively. Title pages will be prepared in manuscript.

Place	Date	Hour	Summary of Events and Information	Remarks and references to Appendices
PETIT RUMES	1/11/18		An uneventful day. Picked up wireless from Paris stating that a satisfactory Armistice had been signed with Austria.	
"	2/11/18		A dull day. Inspite of this our aeroplanes were active, and the enemy AA fire was abnormally high, and the shooting was peculiarly good. Q fire over was continued on the enemy who stated that there was an enemy relief in progress (night 2/3).	
"	3/11/18		A dull day with rain. Situation very quiet through the day. Enemy Anti-aircraft guns reported to be held by 16 Res. & 18 Ersatz Divisions.	
"	4/11/18		Clear day, observation good. Three enemy balloons brought down in flames about 1160. Enemy Artillery quieter than usual/Cherry	
"	5/11/18		Rain throughout the day and night.	
"	6/11/18		Rain throughout day. Situation normal.	
"	7/11/18		Dull day but fine. Enemy artillery very active during afternoon and evening. Two men/exploded in ANTOING. Bavarian Republic Proclaimed	

Army Form C. 2118.

WAR DIARY
or
INTELLIGENCE SUMMARY.

(Erase heading not required.)

Instructions regarding War Diaries and Intelligence Summaries are contained in F. S. Regs., Part II. and the Staff Manual respectively. Title pages will be prepared in manuscript.

Place	Date	Hour	Summary of Events and Information	Remarks and references to Appendices
PETIT RONES	6/11/18		Rain every morning for afternoons, wet moved forward to Mt VELVIN chateau	
Mt VELVIN	7/11/18		Fine day but dull. Feb secured forward across canal to ANTOING. Abdication of Kaiser.	
ANTOING	10/11/18		Weather bright through the day. Kaisers flight to Holland. British at MONS. moved forward to TOURPES	
TOURPES	11/11/18		Good weather. Bn moved forward to ORMEIGNIES. Armistice terms accepted.	
ORMEIGNIES	12/11/18		Cold day but bright. nothing to report.	
"	13/11/18		"	
"	14/11/18		"	
"	15/11/18		"	
"	16/11/18		General Ross inspection of 70th Brigade	
"	17/11/18		Cloudy and dull. nothing to report.	

Army Form C. 2118.

WAR DIARY
or
INTELLIGENCE SUMMARY.
(Erase heading not required.)

Instructions regarding War Diaries and Intelligence Summaries are contained in F. S. Regs., Part II. and the Staff Manual respectively. Title pages will be prepared in manuscript.

Place	Date	Hour	Summary of Events and Information	Remarks and references to Appendices
OTMEIGNE	18.11.18		Nothing to report. Weather cold and foggy	
"	19.11.18		" " " " and fair	
"	20.11.18		" "	
JARDIN	21.11.18		Marched up to Jolain	
"	22.11.18		Weather cold and foggy nothing to report	
"	23.11.18		Nothing to report	
"	24.11.18		"	
"	25.11.18		"	
"	26.11.18		Brigade sports	
"	27.11.18		Nothing to report	
"	28.11.18		"	
"	29.11.18		"	
"	30.11.18		"	

J. M. Wilkinson
Major
Commanding 70th Bde. R.F.A.

CONFIDENTIAL.

WAR DIARY

of

70th Brigade R.F.A.

(Volume 41)

From 1st December 1918.   To 31st December 1918.

WAR DIARY or INTELLIGENCE SUMMARY.

Army Form C. 2118.

DECEMBER

Place	Date	Hour	Summary of Events and Information	Remarks and references to Appendices
JARDIN	1.12.18		Weather fine. Programme of training carried out	
	2.12.18		"D" Battery moved to BRUGELETTE Programme of training carried out.	
	3.12.18		"	
	3.12.18		"	
	4.12.18		Brigade Sports held at BLICQUY (S.11.b)	
	5.12.18		Usual training carried out.	
	6.12.18		"	
	7.12.18		"	
	8.12.18		King's inspection of units of 15th Division near TOURPES. Programme of training carried out.	
	9.12.18		"	
	10.12.18		"	
	11.12.18		Colonel Roberts returned from leave. Usual programme carried out.	
	12.12.18		Major Golan. Leave to for U.K. Programme carried out.	
	13.12.18		"	
	14.12.18		"	
	15.12.18		Usual programme carried out.	
	16.12.18		"	

WAR DIARY or INTELLIGENCE SUMMARY.

DECEMBER Army Form C. 2118.

Place	Date	Hour	Summary of Events and Information	Remarks and references to Appendices
JARDIN	17.12.18		"B" Battery moved forward to CHIEVRES.	
			"A" " " " " BOLIGNIES.	
HORRUES	18.12.18		Brigade and all four batteries moved to HORPUES	
			(Brigade not one length).	
REBECQ	19.12.18		Brigade with four batteries arrive at REBECQ.	
			Finding.	
"	20.12.18		Nothing to report.	
"	21.12.18		" " "	
"	22.12.18		" " "	
"	23.12.18		"B" Battery moves from REBECQ to HENNUYERES.	
"	24.12.18		Nothing to report.	
"	25.12.18		" " "	
"	26.12.18		Brigade football match 70½ goes to 70 R.I.	
"	27.12.18		" " "	
"	28.12.18		Xmas week sports, and meeting parades for all Batteries.	
"	29.12.18		Nothing to report.	
"	30.12.18			
"	31.12.18			

F. G. Ravenur Lieut/Col.
Commanding 70th Bde. R.F.A.

CONFIDENTIAL.

WAR DIARY.

of

70th Brigade R.F.A.

(Volume 42.)

From 1st January 1919.

To 31st January 1919.

Army Form C. 2118.

WAR DIARY
or
INTELLIGENCE SUMMARY.
(Erase heading not required.)

JANUARY 1919.

Place	Date	Hour	Summary of Events and Information	Remarks and references to Appendices
REBECQ	1.1.19 to 5.1.19		At rest. Usual parades and training carried out.	
	6.1.19		Horses classified "A" and "C" Batteries H Quarters & "D" Bty.	
	7.1.19		"	
	8.1.19 & 9.1.19		Nothing to report.	
	10.1.19		Horses classified "B" Battery	
	11.1.19 to 22.1.19		At rest. Usual parades and training carried out.	
	23.1.19		" Horses re-classified.	
	24.1.19		"	
	25.1.19 to 31.1.19		At rest. Usual parades and training carried out.	

F. Robinson L. Col. R.A.
Commanding
70th Brigade R.F.A.

CONFIDENTIAL.

WAR DIARY

of

70th Brigade R.F.A.

(Volume 43)

From 1st February 1919.   To 28th February 1919.

Army Form C. 2118.

WAR DIARY
or
INTELLIGENCE SUMMARY.
(Erase heading not required.)

FEBRUARY Vol 42 1919

Place	Date	Hour	Summary of Events and Information	Remarks and references to Appendices
FARECQ	1.2.19 to 28/2/19		At rest Farecq. usual training and parades.	

Jn. Clothiaue
Major.
Commanding
70th West P.T.A.

CONFIDENTIAL.

WAR DIARY

of

70th Brigade R.F.A.

(Volume 44).

From 1st March 1919.   To 31st March 1919.

Army Form C. 2118.

WAR DIARY
or
INTELLIGENCE SUMMARY.

(Erase heading not required.)

Instructions regarding War Diaries and Intelligence Summaries are contained in F. S. Regs., Part II. and the Staff Manual respectively. Title pages will be prepared in manuscript.

Place	Date	Hour	Summary of Events and Information	Remarks and references to Appendices
REBECQ-ROGNON (BELGIUM)	MARCH 1919.		70th Bde R.F.A. at Rest at REBECQ	

R.A. Symons Lt. RFA
for Major RFA
Comdg 70th Bde RFA

CONFIDENTIAL.

WAR DIARY

of.

70th Brigade R.F.A.

Volume 45)

From 1st April 1919.   To 30th April 1919.

Army Form C. 2118.

WAR DIARY
or
INTELLIGENCE SUMMARY

(Erase heading not required.)

Instructions regarding War Diaries and Intelligence Summaries are contained in F. S. Regs., Part II. and the Staff Manual respectively. Title Pages will be prepared in manuscript.

WO 44

Place	Date	Hour	Summary of Events and Information	Remarks and references to Appendices
REBECQ-ROGNON (BELGIUM)	APRIL 1919		70th Bde R.F.A. at Rest at REBECQ.	

J.W. dePruces Lt RFA
for Major R.F.A.
Comdg 70th Bde R.F.A.

Army Form C. 2118.

70 Bde R.F.A.

Vol 45

WAR DIARY
or
INTELLIGENCE SUMMARY.
(Erase heading not required.)

Instructions regarding War Diaries and Intelligence Summaries are contained in F. S. Regs., Part II. and the Staff Manual respectively. Title pages will be prepared in manuscript.

Place	Date	Hour	Summary of Events and Information	Remarks and references to Appendices
REBECQ-ROGNON. (BELGIUM)	MAY 1919		70th Bde R.F.A. at Rest at REBECQ.	

R.A. Freeman? Lt RFA
for Major R.F.A.
Cmdg 70th Bde R.F.A.

www.ingramcontent.com/pod-product-compliance
Lightning Source LLC
Chambersburg PA
CBHW080900230426

43663CB00013B/2585